THE MISSING COMPETENCY

THE MISSING COMPETENCY

*An Integrated Model for Program Development
for Student Affairs*

*Sharon A. Aiken-Wisniewski,
Rich Whitney, and Deborah J. Taub*

Foreword by Susan R. Komives

STERLING, VIRGINIA

COPYRIGHT © 2021 BY STYLUS PUBLISHING, LLC.

Published by Stylus Publishing, LLC
22883 Quicksilver Drive
Sterling, Virginia 20166-2019

Library of Congress Cataloging-in-Publication Data
The CIP for this text has been applied for.

13-digit ISBN: 978-1-62036-874-9 (cloth)
13-digit ISBN: 978-1-62036-875-6 (paperback)
13-digit ISBN: 978-1-62036-876-3 (library networkable e-edition)
13-digit ISBN: 978-1-62036-877-0 (consumer e-edition)

Printed in the United States of America

All first editions printed on acid-free paper
that meets the American National Standards Institute
Z39-48 Standard.

Bulk Purchases

Quantity discounts are available for use in workshops and for staff development.

Call 1-800-232-0223

Second Edition, 2021

I dedicate this book to my family, Charles and Peg Aiken, Cheryl Aiken,
Alan Wisniewski, and all my friends for their love and patience as I engaged
in writing this book. Additionally, I truly appreciate all my students,
colleagues, and friends who joined me in developing many programs that
offered numerous opportunities to live, learn, and grow.
—Sharon A. Aiken-Wisniewski

I dedicate this book to my parents and brothers, Wilbur, Sheryll, Craig, and Tom,
for all of the support and the combined love we created in our family. Thanks also
to my many students, Scouts, and Arrowmen for the opportunity to share a few
programs that helped to refine my craft along the way.
—Rich Whitney

I dedicate this book to my mother Norma Glosser, husband Steven Taub, and daughter
Rose Taub, with gratitude for their ongoing support. I also thank my good colleagues,
mentors, and students for all that they have taught me.
—Deborah J. Taub

CONTENTS

Programming 4.0: Beyond the Old Story

Many years ago I used to tell a classic story of the young woman who was hosting a family reunion on her farm. She and several of her cousins were talking in the kitchen as she prepared to cook a ham. She methodically cut two inches off each end of the ham, put the ham in a pan, and placed it in the oven. One of her cousins exclaimed, "That is so interesting; that is exactly how I do a ham also." The young woman says, "Well our mothers are sisters, so they must have learned it from Grandma. Let's ask her." They all go out on the porch where Grandma is peacefully rocking in her chair and they say, "Grandma, how come you taught our mothers to cook a ham by cutting pieces off each end?" Grandma paused and thoughtfully replied, "Well, when I was a young bride I had a ham this big [holding her hands about a foot apart] and I had a pan this big [moving her hands in to be about 8 inches apart], so I had to cut off the ends of the ham to fit it into the pan." And they are still cooking their ham this way two generations later—and did not even know why!

This old story provides a useful lesson to examine all the practices, policies, and programs that we continue to perpetuate in student affairs only because we have always done them "that" way. Fortunately, beginning in the 1990s, professionals challenged the unconsidered approach of that old story, particularly informed by useful theoretical models and frameworks and more recently emboldened by applying and assessing specific learning and developmental outcomes expected by our institutions and professional standards. Quality practices in student affairs now strive to design and implement educationally purposeful practices that will have an intended impact on students' learning and development.

This Book

Authors Sharon A. Aiken-Wisniewski, Rich Whitney, and Deborah J. Taub have done a great service to student affairs and to student learning and development with this fine book, *The Missing Competency: An Integrated Model for Program Development for Student Affairs*. The profession owes them great appreciation for returning the foundational competency of programming to our collective attention and providing a contemporary model to implement programs of quality.

Programming 4.0

In so many ways, this book reminds me of the evolution of professional practices in our field over my 50 years of observation. I particularly loved reading the history chapter in this book and identifying with all the models and documents that shaped the evolution of the field. I see roughly four eras in the evolution of programming—all are still with us as we continue to build complexity and refinement in our professional practices. The Programming 1.0 era was the fun-and-games era for programs—typically atheoretical, sometimes serendipitous, and never evaluated. Many of these programs became the campus traditions we continue to this day. Programming 2.0 introduced more thoughtful designs informed by student development theories (e.g., seven-vector frameworks, wellness models) and continue today informed by theoretical insights such as social identity theories and social justice frameworks. Programming 3.0 made programs intentional with the incorporation of student learning and developmental outcomes asserted by the institution, the division of students affairs, or professional guidelines like those of the Council for the Advancement of Standards and other professional associations, *and* included the assessment of those outcomes. We have learned to do intentional design and can do it well. We now live in an era of Programming 4.0, seeking a holistic experience for students that integrates curricular and cocurricular experiences so that all students can experience the institution's learning and developmental outcomes. This approach requires nuances to the programming competency that we must learn, practice, and evaluate. It is, indeed, time to reexamine this missing competency.

The Model

The integrated model for program development (IMPD) in this book is a comprehensive framework for quality professional practice that shows practical considerations in program conceptualization, design, and delivery that apply theory to practice toward intended outcomes. The model reminds me of the observation attributed to Abraham Lincoln, "Give me 6 hours to chop down a tree and I will spend the first 4 sharpening the axe." Doing the hard work to dig deep into the planning needed before program delivery is an art form in itself. This model explicates every stage, particularly the planning stages, so critical to program success. The model is certainly useful in planning and implementing programs but is equally as useful as a heuristic in processing the after-action experience to identify elements for improvement and those that contributed to the success of any event or experience. Readers should photocopy this model and tack it to their bulletin boards for daily reminding and use.

Perspectives on Programming

This book and the IMPD will become a handbook, a guide for facilitators, a stimulus for reflection, and a textbook for student leaders. Professionals using this book and the IMPD should continue to engage in the evolution of programming as a competency. I encourage readers to keep several perspectives in mind in applying the IMPD to contemporary practice.

Make Learning Goals Explicit

It is common now to specify learning and developmental goals or outcomes for each of our programs and policies and most of our practices. These statements provide the "why" to the "what" and "how" of these practices. Formal programs should always have designated learning and developmental goals or outcomes, and these must be shared with the student participants. A decade ago, the American Association of Colleges & Universities did a study of members, determining that 80% of them affirmed their institutions had published learning outcomes (that number is higher now). Interestingly, only 8% thought their students had any idea what those outcome goals were (Hart Research Associates, 2009). It is our responsibility to make sure students know what goals the institution has for them, shape those goals to their personal context, and find resources to learn and develop those goals. Starting every formal program making those goals explicit is a huge step in promoting learning from the experience. It is transparent, ethical, and ensures students see the link between the desired outcome and the experience they are engaging in. If you know a goal you are more likely to accomplish it than if it is a secret. Kudos to the authors of this book for having learning objectives at the start of each chapter, a great way to model your message. Add learning goals to websites, program booklets, program marketing materials, and opening welcome statements when greeting an audience. They should not be a secret.

Map the Whole Environment

It is time to return to the lesson shared in *Learning Reconsidered* (Keeling et al., 2004) and widely discussed when taxonomies of learning and developmental outcomes were advanced: Map the whole college environment to determine where students can engage with experiences to develop those outcomes. Mapping the environment is crucial for several reasons: (a) it finds the strengths of the environment when numerous experiences exist for most students to accomplish a specific outcome; (b) it identifies the weaknesses when few if any experiences exist or when they are not available to most students; (c) it identifies best practices of places implementing this outcome really well who can model and lead organizational change around that outcome; (d) it holds the curriculum and the cocurriculum accountable for educating on those targeted outcomes; and (e) it makes the student experience the center of professional practice, everywhere.

Implement High-Impact Strategies

Those experiences that have the greatest impact on learning and development have been labeled "high-impact practices [HIPs]" (Kuh, 2008). HIPs include activities such as service-learning, capstone projects, study abroad, internships, and living/learning programs. Kuh's (2008) research identified commonly shared elements of HIPs worthy of consideration in the design of all campus programming:

- Significant time and effort allocation
- Meaningful interactions with faculty and peers
- Exposure to different others and different viewpoints
- Frequent feedback
- Opportunities to reflect on learning
- Application of learning to real-world contexts
- Demonstration of competence
- High expectations (list adapted from Kuh, 2008; see also Komives, 2019)

All programs make some kind of impact. Establishing processes in program delivery that require intense time with meaningful interaction involving diverse others and the opportunity to apply the learning to real life with feedback makes a big difference.

Focus on Content

Process is clearly important, both in planning and conducting the event. Indeed, process can become content, with participants learning by how they are engaged in the experience. In our Multi-Institutional Study of Leadership (MSL; see leadershipstudy.net) we learned that the specific platform for a leadership development experience may not matter (e.g., courses, retreats, workshop); it is the content offered in that experience that matters. Students will not learn collaboration or shared leadership (i.e., an intended leadership learning outcome) if the content of the program, in whatever platform, teaches hierarchical, command-and-control methods. Content has to be designed specifically to accomplish the designated outcomes.

Include the Online Learner

It is past time in student affairs practice to revise or enrich our practices to reach and address the needs of the online learner (Budhai, 2019; Crawley, 2012). In many ways, all of our students are online learners; they read articles/resources on the Blackboard or Canvas platforms for classes, they consult your office website for critical resources, they seek your services through email, and on and on. It is past time that we find ways to bring developmentally powerful learning experiences to these learners. I implore today's professionals to challenge their institution's approach to websites. In the early days of websites, over 20 years ago, it seemed we just converted the catalog and student handbooks by locating elements of each in a web version of an organizational chart. If anything, we have not made websites more student friendly or facilitated how they could become portals to a learning experience. We have instead made resources harder to find unless you know already where to look for them. Think of the transformation it would provide to organize some part of the website around learning and developmental goals where students could find self-assessments, readings, resources with links to programs across the campus they could consider, and people to talk with about those experiences. Think about online learners finding online groups to learn specific outcomes. Post videos of campus speakers with online discussion groups. Reframe those websites.

Remember the Ham in the Pan

This book challenges the reader to examine their processes in the planning, delivery, and learning accomplished in every program. It should help each reader identify and develop new competencies needed to do programming really well to create educationally purposeful learning activities for students. This book and this foreword admonish readers to never again put the "ham in the pan" like it has been done without question for 2 decades.

Ask why we do what we do. Does it continue to develop today's students like it did 10 years ago? Whom do the programs we offer leave out? Where is this outcome goal being done well and how can I learn from what that office is doing? Best wishes as you read this book with the open mind of assessing your professional competence in programming and the contributions your programs make to the learning and developmental outcomes you seek in your students.

Susan R. Komives
Professor Emerita
University of Maryland

ACKNOWLEDGMENTS

As we formulated the model and wrote this book, it became clear that our careers offered us many programming experiences. Due to this we want to acknowledge our gratitude to all the organizations that have impacted our understanding of programs and program development. These organizations include but are not limited to University of Maine at Presque Isle, University of Arizona, University of Utah, Weber State University, University of Nevada Reno, DePaul University, University of La Verne, Binghamton University, the University of North Carolina Greensboro, Purdue University, the University of Maryland College Park, Boy Scouts of America, Order of the Arrow, Lions Camp Dat-So-La-Lee, Nevada 4N, American College Personnel Association (ACPA)–College Student Educators International, NASPA—Student Affairs Administrators in Higher Education, National Academic Advising Association (NACADA)—the Global Community for Academic Advising. These organizations offered each of us a true learning experience for program development that we shared in this book.

We want to thank Susan R. Komives for her energies and efforts that resulted in the foreword for this book. Due to her expertise in higher education as a practitioner, leader, and scholar, she has identified the significance of this book for institutional success. Also, the model presented in this book is enhanced by the visual image for the model that Whitney Korda's knowledge in graphic design helped to create. We truly appreciate her expertise.

Finally, we thank Stylus Publishing and our editor, David Brightman, for understanding the importance of this project and accepting our proposal. Through this process of dialogue, writing, and reflection, the integrated model for program development evolved into a tool to share with others engaged in delivering programs.

This book is the product of a question to a faculty electronic mailing list in fall 2017. The email simply asked colleagues to share the resources they use to teach program development in their student affairs graduate programs. The authors of this book as well as hundreds of colleagues were full of anticipation as we waited for replies that would enlighten us on tools, strategies, and techniques. We knew the significance of program development within higher education organizations. Because many of us were engaged in the preparation of future practitioners, administrators, and faculty members through student affairs and higher education administration programs, we were eager to find materials that offered a process without curtailing creativity. Unfortunately, the email responses were limited and sparse. Two people shared a few readings and one shared a design template she had developed based on the work of Claar and Cuyjet (2000). The anticipated bounty of great program development tools so desired by the listserv members was a mirage, a fantasy, an illusion. Or was it? Regardless, it was clear that electronic mailing list members were interested in identifying resources for this topic.

The lack of tools spurred a second email. It asked simply if anyone would like to write a book to address this apparent need. Three people responded and agreed to collaborate to produce this book as a tool for educators, future practitioners, current leaders, students, and all other parties vested in creating programs that deliver success to students, members, and clients.

This book blends the literature relevant to the topic with lived experience to suggest a creative model to guide you in program development. Each chapter offers breadth and depth around the model called the integrated model for program development (IMPD). Before we explore the contents of this book further, let's define *program* in the context of a college campus. A program is "a theoretically based plan, under which action is taken toward a goal within the context of institutions of higher education" (Barr & Keating, 1985, p. 2). Using this definition as a frame, program development focuses on the elements, people, and conditions needed to move the plan from idea to implementation to achieve the goal. This book introduces a stage-based model for program development that is focused on the process to produce a program. Within the stages, techniques and strategies that are necessary to support planning are explained in detail. Finally, guidance for each stage of the model is provided through examples of programs common in student affairs and higher education.

The first two chapters offer context on the topic of program development. Chapter 1 explores the concept of program and programming in higher education as an introduction to the IMPD. This model guides the journey for producing a program by incorporating the stages of defining, planning, monitoring, implementing, and launching into a process that values clarity and detail. Additionally, the IMPD encourages use of theory and scholarly literature as a program moves from inception to completion as well as a reflection stage that incorporates assessment as the planning for the next iteration of the program begins. Chapter 2 shares the complexity of defining *program development* by exploring the literature and the history of the topic over a 50-year period. The next set of chapters encourages the reader and future program coordinator to focus on the process of programming using the model.

Chapter 3 challenges you to ask one basic but strategic question: Why develop this program? Practitioners, leaders, and administrators must focus on the need for the program and know the source or reason that establishes need. This question is answered from a variety of sources such as institutional mission, student data, and/or societal change.

Chapters 4, 5, 6, and 7 introduce specific topics within the IMPD stages that must be addressed in the program development process. Chapters 4 and 5 address topics that concern the program definition stage. Specifically, Chapter 4 defines the terms *goals, objectives*, and *learning outcomes*, which are frequently confused and have been used interchangeably. However, they are in fact different, albeit related, concepts. This chapter presents the differences among these terms, the role of each in program development, and how to write strong goals, objectives, and learning outcomes. Another component critical to program development is the budget. Chapter 5 focuses on fiscal planning for a new program. It will explain strategies and techniques for writing and presenting the budget request. Tips for fiscal accountability will be discussed to demonstrate that the leader is a thoughtful steward of resources as the program is developed and delivered to its intended audience. Once you address the goals, learning outcomes, and budget, it is time to focus on the planning and monitoring stages.

Chapter 6 focuses on planning tasks that achieve the programmatic goals to deliver the activity through a comprehensive spreadsheet and multiple worksheets that create a roadmap. Basically this roadmap offers a clear set of tasks that must be accomplished for planning and monitoring the program. From marketing to training to collaboration, these details identify who, what, where, when, and how as the program starts to take shape. Chapter 7 focuses on the implementation and launch of the program. The team is counting down to delivery of the program and the tasks are assigned to team members over a short period of time. Topics such as training, delegation, and celebration are critical as the program is launched. The launch is an opportunity for celebration of change as a group of people work together to address an institutional need or add a service to support students.

Chapter 8 focuses on the assessment of the program, which moves the process from launch to reflection. The focus is on program success by accomplishing program goals and contributing to the institutional mission. One benefit of properly written objectives and learning outcomes, which are covered in chapter 4, is that these program declarations make assessment of the program considerably more straightforward. The program coordinator and team will know specifically what was to be achieved through the program and identify measurable tools. In essence, you are initiating your assessment plan when you write your goals, objectives, and learning outcomes. Finally, the chapter will describe how to use assessment and evaluation results to improve programs and make decisions about offering the program in the future. Chapter 9 focuses on the stage of program reflection and reviews the complete theory presented in earlier chapters.

In addition to a program development journey, you will find that each chapter begins by articulating learning outcomes for the chapter. Throughout each chapter, you will find figures and tables that offer resources to clarify the IMPD or a specific stage in the model as well as examples from programs in higher education. The book guides you, the reader and program coordinator, from idea to program launch.

Why Would You Open This Book?

Organizations are cultures that are created by people (Bolman & Deal, 2003). Additionally, organizations have a mission statement and strategic goals that establish a direction for the institution, including services and programs (Bender, 2017). At the core of accomplishing these organizational proclamations are well-developed activities and programs. Thus, individuals who engage in program development now or in the future will find this text significant for their work. This individual might be a staff or faculty member or even a student leader. Also, faculty who facilitate courses in student affairs, higher education administration, and leadership preparation programs will find this book a significant resource for their students to understand the process of program development. Through exploring the many facets of program development, it is clear that this book will have relevance at the macro and micro levels of the organization.

As we think of organizations as living organisms, this book offers techniques and strategies for program development that facilitate a thoughtful and vibrant ecosystem (McNair et al., 2016). At the macro level, the organization focuses on obtaining talent in the form of employees. As chapter 1 documents, a recent review of position descriptions used for hiring across the practitioner positions in higher education identifies program development as a key skill set. Applicants for these positions must communicate their experience in developing and delivering programs as well as the assessment process that addresses continuation and sustainability. Whether you are a seasoned professional or new practitioner, this book offers the language to communicate your past accomplishments as well as how you will structure future projects that result in a program to serve students, faculty, and/or staff.

We know that there are some primary audiences that will find this book a must for their professional bookshelf. The first audience is students in graduate preparation programs in student affairs and higher education and new professionals, who can use this book as a primary text in courses focused on program development. As these individuals accept their first position, the information in this book will offer guidance and support.

A second audience is midlevel practitioners in student affairs and higher education—particularly in areas including student activities, residence life, career centers, academic advising, new student programs, service-learning, health promotion, and leadership development. The step-by-step "how to" organization of the book and the inclusion of helpful resources such as planning sheets, checklists, sample budgets, and timeline calculators increase the utility of the book for practitioners. Also, this level of leader is often engaged in comprehensive assessment. Chapter 8 will complement their current skill set.

Third, members of nonprofit organizations would find this volume instructive for basic program design. Similar to many higher education institutions, these organizations have comparable missions that focus on the human condition, limited resources, and a drive to positively impact society. Through the contents delivered to the reader, the question around program design being art, science, or something drawing from both areas is answered with rich description, scholarly references, and strong examples.

How Will You Use This Book?

We also know that program development is a key requirement in most entry and midmanager position descriptions in student affairs. Therefore, this book organizes the literature into one comprehensive volume to inform and guide the work of scholar-practitioners. Beyond a purposeful and well-detailed explanation of program planning, each chapter will open with learning outcomes, provide examples, and offer resources to complement each stage of the model. The overall goal of this book is to provide direction and resources for purposeful program development in higher education and nonprofit organizations at a time when resources are limited but attending to student retention and completion is at a premium.

Conclusion

The goal of this book is to offer a deeper understanding of program development through a model. Whether you are a new professional or a seasoned leader, this volume offers it all. By starting with the definitions, context, and history, the reader has a foundational understanding of this process that is central to supporting the institutional mission in higher education. Next, the book offers a step-by-step model for planning, implementing, and launching a program, from an idea to a proposal with goals, objectives, budget, and timeline with tasks. This volume concludes with stressing the importance and need for assessment as the program continues to develop and accomplish specific goals. Each chapter clarifies program development stages and concepts through program examples. Finally, the authors leave you with resources to complement your program planning process. Overall this book offers guidance as you, the reader and program coordinator, engage in an active and a productive career filled with programs that support the organizational mission for success on all levels.

OVERVIEW OF THE PROGRAM DEVELOPMENT MODEL

Integrated Model for Program Development

After reading this chapter, you will be able to do the following:

1. Define the concept of a program for student affairs practice
2. Explain the need for a program development model for programs that serve students
3. Understand the stages of the integrated model for program development

A college or university campus is an active environment that offers a variety of activities, services, and programs beyond classes that range from a learning abroad fair to a speaker addressing sexual violence prevention to a food drive for the campus food pantry. We know that learning occurs in the classroom through a designated curriculum, but education also is delivered throughout the campus across a variety of experiences that complement and extend the classroom curriculum. These are programs that are delivered by staff and faculty who focus on educating students, often in the area of student affairs. This book focuses on the process of developing programs that deliver information, education, and a sense of belonging to students and the greater campus community in higher education today. The earliest work about program development dates to 1974, and since that time there have been about 20 models presented in various publications. We will address our evolution more in the next chapter; for now, know that we have synthesized this work for you in this new book. Due to the importance of programs and programming in higher education, this book focuses on a model for student affairs practitioners to employ as they accomplish this important responsibility in their campus role. In this chapter you are introduced to the *integrated model for program development* (IMPD), which will guide you, your colleagues, and your students through a process for a successful program outcome. Let's begin this journey by defining *program* and *programming* as well as explaining why we need a process for program development. Then we will explain the IMPD.

Defining *Program* and *Programming*

Programs and programming are the vehicles used by the field of student affairs to contribute to the institutional curriculum. It is through programs that we influence moral and civic learning and student behaviors while students are enrolled on campus (Barr & Keating, 1985; Bryan & Mullendore, 1991; Cooper & Saunders, 2000; Council for the Advancement of Standards, 2009; Cuyjet & Weitz, 2009; Hartwig, 2000; Maki, 2010). These programs connect the students, through our professionals, to the institutional setting and contribute to the ethics and values we hold true as a field and within higher education. The delivery of programs and programming would be better created, implemented, and assessed through systematic program development methods. The purpose of this book is to share a model for program development in the field of student affairs, where programs and programming are so central to the student experience.

Programs (i.e., interventions) are the common denominator of student engagement and learning. "Programmatic intervention is a planned activity with individuals or student groups that is theoretically based and has as its intent the promotion of personal development and learning" (Saunders & Cooper, 2001, p. 310). Within student affairs and many areas of campus life, programs are the standard operating procedure for contributions to the curriculum, and programming is the primary method for the application of student development theory to practice (Evans et al., 2010). These educational practices are primary modes to engage students in the understanding of moral and civic learning and behavior through programs and programming. Although the breadth of functional areas within the field is far-reaching, the standards of application are generally through a variety of programming and campus programs. Programs are so ubiquitous the word itself has multiple connotations and operational definitions. For the purposes of this book, it is important to clearly define *program* and *programming*.

The word *program* was originally used to discuss the student personnel work on a campus (i.e., the division of student affairs) (American Council on Education [ACE], 1937; Lloyd-Jones & Smith, 1938). As the profession grew, expanded, and diversified, it became necessary to delineate that the overall program was an accumulation of programs. To this end, *program* expanded to mean programs and services (e.g., disability resource center), functional areas (e.g., residence life program), departments (e.g., Greek life program), student organizations within departments (e.g., student programming boards), as well as one-time events and activities (e.g., National Coming Out Day) or a series of events (e.g., Black History Month). The series of events could also extend to a semester/quarter speaker series on inclusivity. Get Out the Vote (GOTV) campaigns on campus would be a good descriptor of series and/or the multiplicity approach to programming. Today, we also find even more nuance to campus programs and programming through technology as almost everyone carries a smartphone. *There's an app for that* applies to campus life and campus programming. The intent and purpose of each of these programs carry the common language of meeting student needs or goals through a planned target activity with a specific purpose (Barr & Cuyjet, 1983, 1991). In short, student affairs practitioners delivering programs and an accumulation of activities, especially around a specific theme, is called *programming*.

That student affairs practitioners "spend a significant portion of their working day planning, implementing, and evaluating" (Styles, 1985, p. 181) programs, in all forms and stages, is corroborated throughout our history. Reflecting on 75 years of guidance from the *Student Personnel Point of View* (ACE, 1937), we note program development has been an important part of our history and evolution (Nuss, 2003). The word *program* has expanded and grown since the first synopsis on the role of student affairs on campuses. In the 1937 *Student Personnel Point of View* (SPPV) the word *program* was used to describe student affairs in general, with some references to departments and functional areas. The word *program* was used 51 times in the 1949 SPPV (ACE, 1949). The meaning and function of the word was expanded to include activities (one-time and series) and a directive to include students in these functions. Other foundational and guiding documents of student affairs also refer to programs and programming to describe how student affairs personnel and work fit within the institution and higher education. Jumping forward to *Learning Reconsidered* (Keeling et al., 2004), we find 70 references to programs/programming within 43 pages. Finally, within *Learning Reconsidered 2* (Keeling et al., 2006) references to programs/

programming have tripled (to 267 mentions in 100 pages), further illustrating the centrality these two words have in our work.

It Is All in a Word: Program

We use this one word—*program*—to operationally define a phenomenon within the institution, content areas, activities, semesters, or campus traditions. For these reasons this topic has been difficult to establish as a set protocol (Barr & Cuyjet, 1983, 1991; Barr & Keating, 1985; Cooper & Saunders, 2000; Cuyjet, 1996; Cuyjet & Weitz, 2009; Hurst & Jacobson, 1985; Saunders & Cooper, 2001; Styles, 1985). Over the last 39 years there have been three major definitions surrounding program development. The first describes programs from three perspectives—administrative units, a series of planned interventions, and one-time activities—with each one using a common language to meet student needs or goals with a planned target intervention or purpose (Barr & Cuyjet, 1983, 1991). The second is the most commonly referred to definition within the literature: "a theoretically based plan, under which action is taken toward a goal within the context of institutions of higher education" (Barr & Keating, 1985, p. 2; see also Claar & Cuyjet, 2000; Cooper & Saunders, 2000; Cuyjet, 1996; Cuyjet & Weitz, 2009). Finally, the third major definition says, "Programmatic intervention is a planned activity with individuals or student groups that is theoretically based and has as its intent the promotion of personal development and learning" (Saunders & Cooper, 2001, p. 310; see also Roberts, 2003, 2011). The common pieces of these definitions include being theoretically based and being a plan offering a sense of direction for accomplishing a goal. For the purpose of this book the authors subscribe to the common definition used in the field; a program is "a theoretically based plan under which action is taken toward a goal within the context of institutions of higher education" (Barr & Keating, 1985, p. 2). Now let's turn our attention to one more word—*programming*.

What Is Programming

One derivative of the word *program* is *programming*. Merriam Webster Online Dictionary defines *programming* as "the planning, scheduling, or performing of a program" (Merriam-Webster, n.d.b). When we use this word, which is a noun, it implies action for planning or organizing activities into an educational series. For example, we can incite interest or participation with students and the campus community by saying, "Future programming includes a series of speakers to address the problem of food deserts in the south side of the city." Thus, the word *programming* will be used in this book to describe a planned series of activities that address a theme and focus on college student development. We believe that *program* is defined as "a theoretically based plan, under which action is taken toward a goal" (Barr & Keating, 1985, p. 2). With that in mind, we will discuss why this is important and how we propose one approach the whole process. To begin, we talk about the title of the book and how important program development is to the campus curriculum and learning.

The Missing Competency Is Program Development

The reference to missing competency in the book title is intended to make a point that this key responsibility is missing in current literature and in the development of student affairs practitioners and leaders. The professional competencies that guide the profession are important and on target. The point we are making is that program development is also an important contribution to the campus curriculum/cocurriculum. What seems to be missing to develop effective campus programs and activities that are based on college student development theories, or leadership theories, or learning theories, is a holistic program development model. The opinion that program development is missing emerges from a number of observations. First, the last book that was specifically written about program development in student affairs was published in 1983 (see Barr & Cuyjet, 1983). Second, the evolution of *Student Services: A Handbook for the Profession* illustrates the decline of program/programming terminology. The first edition devoted an entire chapter to program development (see Morrill, 1980), in contrast with the fifth edition in which the concept is merely mentioned within the chapter on community development (Roberts, 2011). Third, at one point, program development was a suggested competency of the student affairs professional (Barr & Keating, 1985; Delworth et al., 1980). The more recent *Professional Competency Areas for Student Affairs Practitioners* (American College Personnel Association [ACPA] & NASPA, 2015) does not highlight program development as a specific competency, but looking at any of the 10 stated competencies, one would find a similar core knowledge base that was described in the Barr and Keating book (1983). In fact, the word *program(s)* occurs 34 times within the ACPA/NASPA (2015) document to illuminate the competencies. These observations support the authors' premise that the concept of program development has moved away from a primary location in the literature to a point of being scattered throughout key documents. Thus, key program development documents can be difficult to find even though programs, programming, and program development are still key responsibilities for careers in student affairs and higher education.

The work staff, students, and faculty do on campus is often through various programs and programming activities. The following analysis of job descriptions demonstrates that the profession is still very program-centric in the application of our work. To illustrate the fact that program development and the functions of programming are important functions we look to the role of student affairs professionals. A study was conducted looking at the jobs advertised in the student affairs field. The three websites included in the study were HigherEdJobs (HEJ; www.higheredjobs.com), the Higher Education Recruitment Consortium (HERC; www.hercjobs.org), and the Careers search engine at Inside Higher Education (IHE; www.careers.insidehighered.com). On the collection days the results of the random student affairs job descriptions available were as follows: HEJ had 566 student affairs job descriptions listed. This was reduced to 234 (41.34%) when the keywords (i.e., program[s], programming, program development) were applied. The same method was applied to HERC and IHE, resulting in 81.13% and 32.09%, respectively. The word *program* appeared in 15.1% of the job titles within the sample. Similarly, 37.20% "required" experience in programs, program development, or programming within the job qualifications. The only things that occurred with consistency were degree requirements and experience in the field. With regard to the ACPA/NASPA competency levels these postings would be categorized as Basic (70), Intermediate (47), and Advanced (28). Programming was the definitional type occurring with the greatest consistency. Within the entire data set programming occurred in 102 (70%) of the job descriptions. This study indicates that as a field we look for people who can develop and deliver programs.

In addition to program development being a key element of position descriptions, we also know that a variety of skill sets that are part of program development are desired by higher education employers. For example, the attention given to assessment and learning outcomes within student affairs as contributions to the curriculum are primarily at the program and programming levels on each campus (Bresciani, 2009; CAS, 2009; Hartwig, 2000; Keeling et al., 2006; Maki, 2010; Suskie, 2009). Also, supervisors need skills that focus on human resources, budgeting, and the application of technology. All these skill sets are paramount to a comprehensive model that focuses on program development. Due to the reduction of information on program development or program development models in more recent literature as well as limited specific mention of program development in competency documents offered by many professional organizations for student affairs fields, this book will attend to the competency of program development through modeling and discussing a variety of skill sets needed by practitioners, students, and faculty. Thus, the focus of this book, the IMPD, is significant because programming and program development are key responsibilities for many campus positions and careers.

The Heart of the Program

The heart of every program is centered on people. Up to this point we have been focusing on the words *program, program development,* and *programming.* While the how and what of program development are key, we have to remember the why is centered on the people involved. Even the definition we use delineates the how and what of programming supports the *why* we do the *planned activity with individuals or student groups.* The work throughout this book assumes the understanding that programs, and programming, are for the enhancement of learning and engagement for our key people: the students, the learners, the participants. The focus on the people does not begin and end with the student only. Program developers are the people using the IMPD. We will discuss how these people are sometimes faculty and staff, and at times students can perform this role as well. The team leadership and collaborative approach to creating and implementing programs is dependent on the strengths and talents of the people involved.

Elements of the IMPD

This chapter presents an integrated and contemporary model for program development that brings all of the elements and skill sets together from start to finish. There is so much more to the program development process than what the participant sees. In programming language, the final payoff would be the perfect implementation on the day of the event. The truth of the matter is that there is a lot more to the process before the event occurs or the new service opens the doors. The elements of programming are many and require a variety of skills to move from an immediate need to the delivered program and the end of the project. Let's start developing an understanding of the program development process by exploring the stages of the IMPD.

For those learners who like to see all of the steps in one place we have listed them here as a preview of the stages in the model. Then in each of the subsections those internal stages will be presented and then explained to provide context and show their contributions to the model. Finally, specific chapters in the book will offer greater depth on stages and skill sets required for these stages. It is important to understand that the model and process are dynamic and interactive, which means that a detail or an activity for one program might be listed in one stage but another program might add that activity to a different stage. Basically, the details for the model and stages along with key elements of each stage are offered as a guide for comprehensive program planning, as shown in the following:

Program Definition
- Needs assessment
- Campus setting
- Learning outcomes
- Target population
- Program goals
- Theoretical frame
- Planning team

Program Planning
- Target date
- Backdating schedule
- Budget
- Assessment planning
- Learning outcomes
- Rollout plan
- Collateral
- Printing
- Talent contracts and demands
- Staffing plan
- Marketing plan
- Communications plan
- Location/programming space
- Training sessions
- Risk management

Implementation—Prelaunch
- Detailed time sequence
- Last-minute checklist
- Paperwork that may be required
- Travel details, airport plans, and contact numbers

Program Launch
- Preliminary deliverables
- Implementation

- Staffing schedule
- Final checks
- Day of event
- Quick notes about what we could do better/what worked immediately
- Another quick walk-through and check to make sure supplies are in place
- Calls to check on elements that were late or that were unfortunately missing
- Checks on final placements of equipment
- Scan doors to the venue for security now that everyone has arrived
- Quick reorganization of check-in paperwork. Do it now.

Program Monitoring (or Program Control)
- Counting, accounting, recording
- Formative evaluation
- Constant monitoring
- Plans B, C, D, . . .
- Risk management
- Unplanned evaluations
- Attractive nuisances

Program Reflection
- Cash from event
- Receipts
- Assessment completed
- Monetary accounting
- Contract closeout
- Recognition
- Reporting
- After-action report
- Administrative decisions for future plans

Now that you are starting to develop an understanding of the stages with specific components, we offer an illustration (Figure 1.1) of how the stages are integrated into the model.

Figure 1.1 communicates the potential flow among the stages. The entire model sits on a theoretical foundation. This foundation refers to the theory that will ground the program you are developing for your campus. We do not articulate which theory here on purpose. Your theory of choice will become part of your discovery in the beginning of your program ideas. The first phase of the model is the program definition stage.

Figure 1.1. Integrated model for program development.

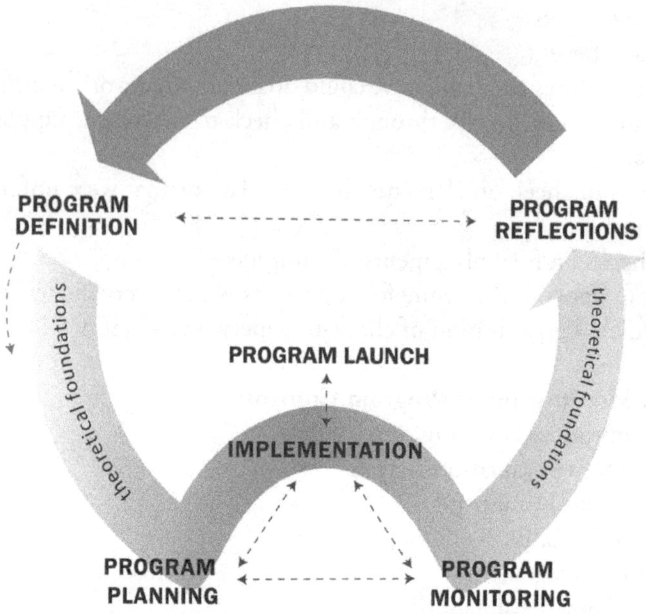

Note. Image of model created by Whitney Korda, w.inc. digital.

Program Definition

It all starts here at program definition. It is the point of an idea emerging that would be addressed through a program. This is where we ask questions. Is there a need for this program? Are we addressing the campus mission with this program? Is there an intervention for this program? The scope of a program ranges from educational to social to wellness, with possible overlap being a bonus. This stage is the 30,000-foot level of looking at the program. The IMPD is fluid and you cannot always see the overlap between the stages easily. This is purposeful. As the program coordinator (or the program committee) starts to mold the big picture, you will naturally begin to move to the planning stages. It is important that your committee composition represents your campus populations and that many perspectives are helping to shape your programmatic definitions and planning. The people on your committee will be the voices you need for inclusive and welcoming programs that meet the needs of all of your participants. Your attention to the underlying college student development theory and framework will also begin to take more shape in your program. The movement from definition to planning will become more and more tangible as you home in on the learning outcomes and population. Considering your assessment plans, you can move from learning outcomes to a fuller and richer conversation on the whole assessment plan. This may seem like you are doing both definition and planning at the same time. The answer is that you might be doing just that, which is one example of the fluidity of the model and process. The list of the programming elements within this stage are outlined in the following:

Program Definition
- Needs assessment
- Campus setting
- Learning outcomes
- Target population
- Program goals
- Theoretical frame
- Planning team

As was mentioned earlier, the program definition stage will engage elements of the program planning stage in this model. It is natural movement between the stages. Chapter 3 offers information on the *why* components with regard to needs and data sources that are relevant to this stage. The program moves from program definition into the program planning stage as the needs for the program are affirmed and a generalized program vision transitions to specific details.

Program Planning

It is impressive what a committed committee and group of students, staff, and faculty can put together in the short span of a semester, or a quarter. Never doubt the power of intention and the commitment of a group of people. We have all heard the Margaret Mead quote, "Never doubt that a small group of thoughtful, committed citizens can change the world; indeed, it's the only thing that ever has" (quoted in Keys, 1982, p. 79). We have found this to be true. This power of intention is amazing, and it can work for a program as well. We have all had experiences with the program that included inception to implementation within the short weeks of a semester/quarter. A caveat here is that the hurry-and-plan mentality is likely part of the cause to overlook or disregard the need for a program development model/system. "We don't have time for all that planning stuff, it takes too much time" is a dangerous thought pattern. In order to plan a great program it will be helpful to heed the construction maxim of "measure twice and cut once."

The more attention you have spent in planning, organizing files, and dealing with details, the more relaxed you will be at this stage. It is in this stage that you will need something from the collaborative electronic file and you do not want to be searching through an electronic junk drawer looking for that file "I just put in here last night." Trust us, it has happened to all of us.

This is likely the longest part of your planning process. It will probably take the most meetings and it will take the most people power you can put together. The first tool that should be used is a "backdater." We have included a general backdater in the appendix to help you with your creation of a plan. A backdating plan starts with the end in mind and works backward to determine the lead time for each of your program target goals, program deliverables, and of course the program launch. This planning activity helps to create the deliverables, actions, and important dates that you need to hit prior to the event. The backdater we have supplied is generalized and we have included many things for you to consider. Depending on the size of your program you may need fewer items or you may find out you need more. Certain campus or city policies, laws, and regulations may add unique items to the detail of your overall plan. Chapter 4 offers greater detail on program goals, objectives, and outcomes. Chapter 5 addresses budget essentials for you and your program.

There are many computer programs and apps now that can help with your planning process. The use of a Google Drive folder or some other common repository for your committee work will help with transparency and smooth sailing. The key to the online collaborative folder is to keep "electronic hygiene" in mind. Spend some time creating folders, naming conventions, and organization methods for your collaborative dropbox. Create a history file in each section so you can archive the old plans and keep the great thinking that took place. Keep the most recent, dated (with creation and revision notations), and page numbered. This little bit of electronic hygiene will keep your collaborative files from looking like your family junk drawer and contribute to an organized process. The list of the programming elements for the planning stage within this model are outlined in the following:

Program Planning
- Target date
- Backdating schedule
- Budget
- Assessment planning
- Learning outcomes
- Rollout plan
- Collateral

- Printing
- Talent contracts and demands
- Staffing plan
- Marketing plan
- Communications plan
- Location/programming space
- Training sessions
- Risk management

As this list indicates, there are many details to this stage in the IMPD. The creation of a holistic program includes attending to all populations that you will serve through your programs and activities. Universal design helps to examine all entry points into the program for physical disabilities, learning styles, and cultural nuances. During this time you will want to think about the sequencing of your program as well. You will want to be attentive to how you order things to help with understanding, timing, and readiness for learning (Bloom & Krathwohl, 1956; Kolb, 2015; Seemiller & Whitney, 2020; Whitney et al., 2016)

Chapter 6 engages with other details of planning, such as the people who plan a program, the development of a timeline, and initiating a marketing plan to guarantee participation. The next stage after planning is implementing and launching the program.

Launching Stage—Implementation

There are always last-minute things to do prior to launch. It will just work out that you cannot take care of some part of the program and the launch until the week, day, morning, or hour before the program begins. Equate this to leaving on a trip. Think of all the things you cannot do until the last minute, the morning of, or the last few hours before your flight. Implementation will require its own checklist of details, logistics, and contact phone numbers. This seems like a prestage or a ministep between the planning and the launch, but it is vital. Take the time to plan for the last-minute details. The list of the programming elements in the prelaunch step are outlined in the following:

Implementation—Prelaunch
- Detailed time sequence
- Last-minute checklist
- Paperwork that may be required
- Travel details, airport plans, and contact numbers

Program Launch

Project management calls this stage "project execution." We did not like the sound of that stage and thought it was much more appropriate in student affairs to "launch a program." The launch is often referred to in programming and program development as the "day of," meaning the day of the event. The day of will be hectic. The whole event needs to be scripted for a smooth delivery. Written plans and a procedure will help reduce the confusion and we suggest a series of worksheets in a spreadsheet to support a clear path. If you can write out the steps that everyone will need to follow, or at least be aware of, it will help reduce the word of mouth interpretations. Points will not be forgotten in haste if you have the plan printed and posted. It is your planning that will eliminate a hectic situation and reduce chaos so you can launch a great program. How you organize your participation on the launch day is important and should be included in your planning. If you and various members of your team are social individuals, you will want to be in the front of the room greeting people as they show up to your program and seeing their initial reactions. If you and team members are naturally structural or analytical, it is likely you love all of the elements of implementing to watch the event emerge. Your plans were set a week before, and you are just as happy being in the background making sure the details are attended to for everyone else. Know your team and make sure appropriate assignments are made that address member skills for a smooth launch. The day of the program will be spent on walk-through, triple checking the security plans, and ensuring that everything is moving forward. The list of the programming elements within this stage are outlined in the following:

Program Launch and Implementation
- Preliminary deliverables
- Implementation
- Staffing schedule
- Final checks
- Day of event
- Quick notes about what we could do better/what worked immediately
- Another quick walk-through and check to make sure supplies are in place
- Calls to check on elements that were late or that were unfortunately missing
- Checks on final placements of equipment
- Scan doors to the venue for security now that everyone has arrived
- Quick reorganization of paperwork that was used for check-in and the launch. Do it now.

It is purposeful that implementation is accomplished with monitoring of the events, activities, and details not forgotten. The launch was really liftoff and now we are in the process of delivering and monitoring the program at the same time. This ministep between the kickoff and the monitoring will guide immediate considerations and alterations at various times in the future. As the first iteration of the program is delivered, the monitoring stage will appear first informally, with brief notes written while the program is in motion, and then more formal evaluation through an assessment plan. Chapter 7 offers information on work flow, training activities, and team celebration strategies as the vision becomes reality on your campus.

Program Monitoring

Monitoring happens from the minute the program starts, through the secondary implementation, and continues until the last participant leaves. It is all planning until the director says, "Action!" and "Voila, we are in monitoring." This phase is where plan B may become a reality and has to be fulfilled. Monitoring is being able to react on the fly when an unknown or unplanned variable suddenly appears in the middle of your program. Weather conditions (that happen midlaunch and unexpectedly) would be a monitoring event. Power outages are dealt with in monitoring. The fortunate benefit of having more people show up than you were ready for and needing to adjust the check-in line or use alternative methods to check people in. The food delivery is not going as planned. An attractive nuisance in programming is some element you thought might add ambiance, like a lake or a stream, but then it turns into a nuisance because of the noise or distraction it creates for your program. These examples are a bit extreme to make the point, but you need to be ready for almost anything. The list of the programming elements within this stage are outlined in the following:

Program Monitoring (or Program Control)
- Counting, accounting, recording
- Formative evaluation
- Constant monitoring
- Plans B, C, D, . . .
- Risk management
- Unplanned evaluations
- Attractive nuisances

Counting, accounting, and recording are key elements of the monitoring stage. During the monitoring stage of your program you will want to ensure that you remember the numbers. Counting seems trivial, but it is not. Imagine the difference in impact between these statements: "There were a lot of people there; the room was packed" and "The attendance was great; we had 213 people in that room. We were just under the fire code limits." Your vice president will be much more impressed with 213 (a number) than just being told, "The room was packed." Accounting is vital. Control over the money and the accounting during the event is a must. The campus professional should at all times know and be responsible for the money. Collecting money at the end is vital as well. Do not give this responsibility to anyone else. The same caution goes for the departmental P-card or purchasing card. Recording is a reminder to make notes somehow throughout the monitoring. Some ways this can be done include sending yourself text messages with notes; taking pictures of things that worked or did not work; or keeping an Evernote file with notes. You will be happy you took the time to make notes and archive some things while you were in the moment. Relying on your memory will be frustrating later when you have a list of 20 things you thought you would remember but that just seem to escape you later. Chapter 7 will offer further information on the monitoring stage and chapter 8 will provide support for the assessment plan that is another form of monitoring for future reports.

Reflection Stage

The program is not "done" until all of the final reports are created, analyzed, reported, discussed, and a meeting has taken place. The decision to move forward for next year rests in the palm of your closeout hands. A poor closeout during your reflection stage and reporting will be the last thing that people will remember. The sponsor that was vital for making the program happen but did not receive a follow-up report, a thank-you note, or some point of contact after the fact will have a bitter taste in their mouth when it comes time to give money or product next time. The reflection stage is probably the hardest of the stages in which to keep your energy focused. The adrenaline rush of planning and launching the event will be gone. It is likely that the next responsibility for your position is waiting for your attention. The more attention you have spent in planning the details, launching the program, and instituting the monitoring activities, the more prepared and relaxed you will be in the reflection stage. The list of the programming elements within this stage are outlined in the following:

Program Reflections
- Cash from event
- Receipts
- Assessment completed

- Monetary accounting
- Contract closeout
- Recognition
- Reporting
- After-action report
- Administrative decisions for future plans

The arc over the top of the model (see Figure 1.1) also has some meaning. Reflection is about looking back at the program and closing it out for this iteration. This phase also sets into motion some thinking about the next iteration of the program, or if there will be a next time. This is the administrative review to address the viability of the program. So this arc across the top is to represent one iteration of the program to the next, which could be next semester, next year, every 2 years, or whenever. The program development model is truly a cyclical process.

There are cross-sectional interactions between four of the stages that are important to note. The dotted lines represent the connections between the stages that are not sequentially adjacent. Program definitions and program reflection stages are related as the opening and the closing stages of the model. The mission and purpose will be important at both ends. The program has to have a sound basis for need, intervention, interaction, capacity, and utility. We want to spend our time and resources on a program that meets a purposeful need among the student population on campus. This section is connected to the program reflection stage because so much of the ending pieces have to be considered, planned for, and implemented prior to the beginning of another iteration of the program. If we do not attend to the budget, assessment plan, marketing, and theoretical foundations in the definitions phase, we will not have the data or structure to complete these weeks or months later after the event.

The other cross-functional alignment between the program planning and the program monitoring stages straddle the implementation and the program launch stages. Remember, the key stage of program planning sets the definitions into play: the structure of the working committee, the roles each play in the program, and the operationalization of the whole program process/structure. It follows the guiding documents and the vision of the program. While we are moving through the planning and implementation phases there will naturally be program monitoring and formative evaluations happening. Without solid planning and a sense of trust, structure, accountability, and process, the monitoring will be a disaster. The planner has to delegate the action and the responsibility for the program. Otherwise, when an anomaly happens, or a computer glitch, or the dropping of some balls along the way, everyone will be looking around to see "who is in charge here?" Planning gives you the ability to monitor the program as it is happening, which the IMPD advocates for throughout. The alignment and symbiotic relationship between the stages in this model are intentional for success of the initial program as well as future iterations. Chapters 3 through 8 offer opportunities to see the interaction between the stages of this model. Chapter 9 provides a deeper perspective on the reflection stage.

Conclusion

This chapter explored the terms *program* and *programming* in the current context of student affairs and higher education. A *program* is defined as "a theoretically based plan, under which action is taken toward a goal" (Barr & Keating, 1985, p. 2). Even though this term and definition are relevant to the mission of any campus, and both appear in many staff and some faculty position descriptions as necessary skills, the current literature base presents minimal tools to develop a successful program. Due to the importance of programs in higher education, the authors offer the IMPD as a tool for developing programs to address students' needs and expectations in 21st-century higher education. This model emerged through the lived experiences of the authors as well as a comprehensive review of program development models used in student affairs for the last 50 years, which are presented in chapter 2.

Chapter 2 offers an historical perspective on program development models used in higher education. This chapter will document a long and vibrant history of program development for the college environment. The authors understand that it might not be of interest to all readers but we include it to chronicle the use of theory and models for program development that have been part of the higher education landscape for many years. It also points to the importance of planning and process in program development.

Chapters 3 through 9 offer depth and detail to apply to each stage of the IMPD. It is this rich detail that will offer direction for new practitioners planning their first program. Seasoned practitioners and leaders will appreciate the focus on monitoring, assessment, and reflection for staging future iterations of the event. Finally, all individuals involved in program planning and development will appreciate the interaction between each stage that offers direction without limiting how certain elements emerge in specific plan for their respective campus. Throughout you will find tools, strategies, and ideas that are shared for your success in program development as well as the holistic success of your students.

EVOLUTION OF PROGRAM DEVELOPMENT

After reading this chapter, you will be able to do the following:

1. Identify the major contributors to the history of program development
2. Understand the history and evolution of program development models in student affairs
3. Synthesize the important parts of a program model

The key to success often starts with a goal, intended outcomes, and a planned course of action to achieve the goal and outcomes. This book on program development is, in essence, a type of program for all of you. Hence, our first chapter focuses on goals, outcomes, and a plan by defining key terms and outlining a model for program development. In the first chapter, we moved quickly to share the goal and key deliverable of this book, the IMPD. The purpose of the first chapter was to offer an overview of program development that is based on this comprehensive model for delivering programs, services, and events that contribute to student success.

Why do programs within student affairs warrant such attention that program development models are needed? The answer to this question is significant for not only this chapter but also this book. Campus programs and programming are a contribution to the overall institutional curriculum. The earliest foundational documents of the field address the need for programs and programming (ACE, 1937, 1949). This is reinforced in the attention to how student affairs contributes to learning and the curriculum in both volumes of *Learning Reconsidered* (Keeling et al., 2004; Keeling et al., 2006). The theories of college student development that create the common vernacular of our profession also create meaningful programs for experiential learning for our students (Evans et al., 2010). The book *Where Colleges Fail* by the progenitor of college student development theory Nevitt Sanford (1967) actually has the subtitle of *A Study of the Student as a Person*, discussing how we support students through challenge and attending to their readiness to learn. Programming and program development helps to operationalize this learning. All of this learning takes place through real life and a model that directs the use of theory as we define, plan, launch, monitor, and ultimately reflect, a system that provides guidance for achieving the goal and outcomes of a program. Thus, a model for program development offers a process for successful delivery of curriculum within the area of student affairs. But the IMPD is not the first model to inform student affairs practice.

This chapter offers models that informed our work as we developed the IMPD as well as the work of many leaders and practitioners in student affairs for the last 50 years. It is a brief, historical overview, which suggests models of program development previously used in student affairs. The purpose of this chapter is to take a short pause from explaining stages and key elements of the IMPD to honor the pioneers of program development in student affairs. Program development spans more than 45 years and 20 models, which begs the question: Why are there no books or conversations on this subject?

We provide an extensive review of all of the models pertaining to program development in the history of student affairs. We are pretty proud of the fact that this is the *only* place in the student affairs literature where you can find all of the models in one place. There are 21 models that date back to 1974. We used this research on all of the models to synthesize the components into a more contemporary model for program development for today's campus professional—the IMPD. In addition to offering a historical overview for those engaged in program development, students completing a literature review that would include program development will find that this chapter offers a comprehensive understanding of programming through specific models. Regardless of your engagement with program development at this time, the models offered in this chapter provide historical perspective to programming.

Brief History of Program Development

The sentiment that student affairs practitioners "spend a significant portion of their working day planning, implementing, and evaluating" (Styles, 1985, p. 181) programs is corroborated by many authors over time. The foundational documents of the student affairs profession show there is significant history of programs, program development, and programming (ACE, 1937, 1949; Nuss, 2003).

Jumping forward to more recent publications, we find that *Learning Reconsidered* (Keeling et al., 2004), and *Learning Reconsidered 2* (Keeling et al., 2006) refer to programs/programming often (70 and 267 times, respectively). The Council for the Advancement of Standards in Higher Education (CAS, 2019) provides tremendous resources for implementing programs and helps to outline important considerations for the implementation of divisional, departmental, and some programmatic functions on campus. However, CAS does not present a particular program development model. This is not to minimize or dismiss the use of CAS in our programming work. The CAS standards are operational and should be used as a formative evaluation tool to improve or expand divisional/departmental programs (Bryan & Mullendore, 1991; CAS, 2019).

The following descriptions provide a short explanation of each model, and how they fit into the evolution of the programming development models. A chronological listing of the 21 models has also been included here as a general guide.

Chronology of Program Development Models

1. 1973—The ecosystem model/Western Interstate Commission for Higher Education (WICHE) (Banning & Kaiser, 1974)
2. 1973—Seven-dimensional model of outreach potential (Drum & Figler, 1973)
3. 1974—Schematic for change (Lewis & Lewis, 1974)
4. 1974—The cube (Morrill et al., 1974)
5. 1976—Future of student affairs (Miller & Prince, 1976)
6. 1976—Student services program development model–Linear model (Moore & Delworth, 1976)
7. 1976—The ecosystem model (Aulepp & Delworth, 1976)
8. 1978—Ecomapping (Huebner & Corazzini, 1978)
9. 1983—Barr and Cuyjet five-step model (Barr & Cuyjet, 1983)
10. 1985—Barr and Keating model—Cube and WICHE models (Barr & Keating, 1985)
11. 1985—Theoretical and conceptual foundations for program development–Modified cube model (Hurst & Jacobson, 1985)
12. 1985—Model for future program development (Styles, 1985)
13. 1989—Health and wellness model (Mosier, 1989)
14. 1989—Student leadership program model—(Roberts & Ullom, 1989)
15. 1991—Program development six-step model (changed the five-step model) (Barr & Cuyjet, 1991)
16. 1996—Cuyjet model—Modified Barr and Cuyjet six-step model (Cuyjet, 1996)

17. 2001—Saunders and Cooper program model (Saunders & Cooper, 2001)
18. 2001—Community-building program model (Roberts, 2011)
19. 2006—Comprehensive leadership program model (Haber, 2006)
20. 2009—Typical process of program planning and implementation—(Cuyjet & Weitz, 2009)
21. 2011—Formal leadership program model (Haber, 2011)

Some of these models get confusing because they have similar names, or the same name in some cases. Hopefully the chronological list and brief synopses of the important models will help you understand their basic contributions to program development as well as the interactive relationships between models.

The Ecosystem Model for Campus Design

WICHE presented this model in 1973 (see Figure 2.1). The model addresses the whole of campus life to examine the interrelationships of the different populations on campus—students, staff, and faculty (Banning & Kaiser, 1974). Although it is not about creating specific programs for any particular population, it does provide a methodology for creating change. This seven-step model discusses the concept of an ecosystem—or the interaction between campus partners and the resulting mutually beneficial change (Banning & Kaiser, 1974).

The presumption of student affairs and programs up to this point seemed to be that our work was more reactive than proactive. At the time student personnel work was thought to help the student adjust to college and campus life. The WICHE ecosystem model was developed to address the complexity of people coming together on campus at three different levels—macro, micro, and individual life space (WICHE, 1973). The macro level involves the entire campus organization, whereas the micro level is concerned with specific groups on campus. The life-space level addresses individuals, including the need for assessment within groups (Banning & Kaiser, 1974). The seven steps of the basic design are also provided.

Figure 2.1. The ecosystem model: Designing campus environments.

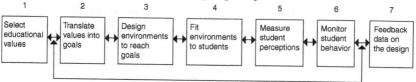

Note. This rendering adapted from Banning & Kaiser (1974).

1. Designers, in conjunction with community members, select educational values.
2. Values are translated into specific goals.
3. Environments are designed containing mechanisms to reach the stated goals.
4. Environments are fitted to students.
5. Student perceptions of the environments are measured.
6. Student behavior resulting from environmental perceptions is monitored.
7. Data on the environmental design's success and failures, as indicated by student perceptions and behavior, is fed back to the designers in order that they may continue to learn about student environment fit and design better environments (Banning & Kaiser, 1974).

The Cube

The cube model seems to have taken a primary role in the literature over the years. The cube (Morrill et al., 1974) was originally developed to describe the functions of counselor interventions within a special edition entitled "The Dimensions of Counseling" in the February 1974 issue of the *Personnel and Guidance Journal*. The issue presented Morrill et al.'s renowned cube and all of the included articles operationalized or described the use of the model.

The cube in Figure 2.2 illustrates a three-dimensional model categorizing the broad range of interventions to consider in the counseling process: target, purpose, and method. In the original model the target comprises (a) individual, (b) primary group, (c) associational group, and (d) institution or community. The purpose of the intervention included the definitional attributes of remediation, prevention, and development. Finally, the delivery methods are direct service, consultation, and media. The original authors suggested that any intervention needs to answer the questions of who or what (target), why (purpose), and how (method) (Schuh & Triponey, 1993). The initial article on the cube model addressed the importance of assessment before the implementation of any intervention or program. The assessment must look at the needs of the person/group, the environment, and institutional conditions and resources (Morrill et al., 1974). In their description of the cube model in the *New Directions in Student Services* monograph on programming, the authors (Cooper & Saunders, 2000) acknowledged the lack of assessment as an explicit part of the cube model and process. They suggested the original authors had assume that assessment is part of the process but they did not specifically address the topic. Perusal of the original article clearly shows that Morrill et al. (1974) acknowledged the need for assessment,

Figure 2.2. The cube model.

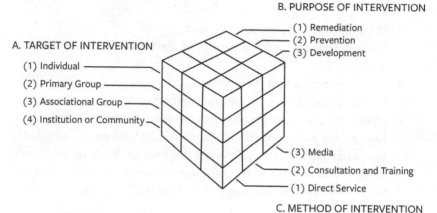

B. PURPOSE OF INTERVENTION
— (1) Remediation
— (2) Prevention
— (3) Development

A. TARGET OF INTERVENTION

(1) Individual ———
(2) Primary Group ———
(3) Associational Group ——
(4) Institution or Community ——

— (3) Media
— (2) Consultation and Training
— (1) Direct Service

C. METHOD OF INTERVENTION

Note. This rendering adapted from Morrill et al. (1974).

which connects to their counseling paradigm. What Cooper and Saunders (2000) might have been addressing is that assessment is not explicitly labeled within the 10 elements on the cube illustration. Like the ecosystem model discussed in the previous section, the cube model is not overtly presented as a student affairs program development model per se, but like the previous model it does provide a substantial basis from which program development within student affairs has evolved. In most cases, this model is simply referred to as the cube (Evans, 1987; Kuh, 1999; Miller & Prince, 1976).

The Ecosystem Model

The name of this model appears to be the same as the first one on the list. They are in fact different. The year 1976 seems to have been a big year in the expansion of three program development models due to multiple task force teams receiving grants to develop program development models for campus (Moore & Delworth, 1976, Fig. 3). The literature gets quite confusing during this time due to the fact that one author participated in two models that were both associated with WICHE (Aulepp & Delworth, 1976; Moore & Delworth, 1976). Two of the models have similar sounding names that originate from the ecosystems approach to college student personnel work at the time. These two are the ecosystem model (Aulepp & Delworth, 1976) based on the 1973 model created by the WICHE task force and the eco-mapping model (Huebner & Corrazzini, 1978).

The ecosystem model introduced a five-stage model that was based on the seven-stage model of the ecosystem model for campus design (Banning &

Kaiser, 1974; WICHE, 1973). This training document addresses the person/ environment interactions for micro-level projects, (Aulepp & Delworth, 1976). Remember, the micro level of ecosystem designs is the on-campus groups (Banning & Kaiser, 1974). The ecosystem model design philosophy is based on eight assumptions (Aulepp & Delworth, 1976):

1. There are multiple stimuli (e.g., physical, chemical, biological, and social) impinging on the student within the campus environment.
2. There is a transactional approach between the student and the campus environment.
3. Students are active choice-making agents who can resist, transform, or nullify campus environmental influences.
4. Each student has the capacity for a spectrum of behaviors that must be considered when designing growth and development opportunities.
5. Students will attempt to cope (positively or negatively) with the educational environment they experience.
6. Due to the diversity of students, it is important to create a variety of campus subenvironments.
7. Every campus has a design (i.e., culture), whether it is intentional or unintentional. Successful campus design depends on participation by all (e.g., students, faculty, staff, administration, trustees, and regents).
8. The campus design depends on buy-in from a variety of campus levels (students, staff, faculty, administration, and trustees).

From the name—the ecosystem model—we can see the ecological perspective as a given as well as the transactional nature of helping the student adjust to their new environment. The authors suggested that college student development was concerned with helping students adjust to their new campus environment. It is important to note the role of assessment for topic areas (i.e., need), which is the first role of the newly established planning team, per the model.

Some authors (Cuyjet, 1996) have attributed Aulepp and Delworth with creating the ecomapping model of 1976. Technically this is incorrect; Aulepp and Delworth did create an ecosystem model in 1976 but it followed the same naming convention as the earlier WICHE (1973) model. In a program development chapter on residential life and housing, a chapter by Schuh and Triponey (1993) properly outlines the WICHE ecosystem model with the 1973 report, the 1974 article, and the 1976 report by Aulepp and Delworth. The confusion here may be that Styles (1985) discussed how "ecomapping can occur at three different levels" (p. 186), describing the macro, micro, and life-space levels of design. As referenced earlier, there was an additional 1976 model in the literature called the eco-mapping model, which is discussed next.

Eco-Mapping

To further add to the confusion, another model has a similar name, but is indeed another model on the list. The eco-mapping model is also based on campus ecology theory (Huebner & Corazzini, 1978). Similarly, this is approached as the intentional designing of campus environments and how they contribute to student-faculty interactions. The term *mapping* (Morrill et al., 1980, p. 69) describes the process of matching, or the identification of mismatches, within the needs of the student in the campus environment. The 10-step process of the eco-mapping model acknowledges that the assessment and intervention processes use multiple methods for a complete understanding of the environment.

1. Obtain, sanction, and establish an onsite design team
2. Chart the topography
3. Assess characteristics of constituents
4. Identify apparent matches and mismatches
5. Validate matches and mismatches
6. Identify behaviors used to cope with apparent and real mismatches
7. Feedback information to the onsite design team
8. Evaluate where changes need to and can be made
9. Plan and implement program and environmental interventions
10. Assess the intervention and continue feedback (Huebner & Corazzini, 1978)

This model is based on the ecosystem theory of college student development, but we can see a different approach to deciding on, implementing, and measuring the effectiveness of interventions. The action steps of the eco-mapping process occur in steps 7 through 9 when the planning team considers the data and implementation occurs. This could be in the form of "system changes . . . or program development activities" (Morrill et al., 1980, p. 70). The addition of steps and the multiple modalities of data collection were acknowledged as time-consuming and hard to apply. This may have resulted in the lower adoption or use rate by the field. This model is probably more indicative of creating a student personnel program (i.e., division of student affairs) on campus congruent with campus culture and institutional mission.

However, it is included here due to the number of inconsistencies in the nomenclature of the literature to date.

Linear Model

Another program development model introduced in 1976 is called the student services program development model, or the linear model for short (Moore & Delworth, 1976). Here we have a new name for the model, but we find that an author has created and written on two of our models, and in the same year: the previous ecosytem model (Aulepp & Delworth, 1976) and now this linear model (Moore & Delworth, 1976). This five-stage model was also an adaptation of the 1973 WICHE ecosystem model and helped to operationalize the Morrill et al. (1974) cube model. According to the authors (Moore & Delworth, 1976), this particular model was adopted by WICHE for "testing and refinement through on-site campus application" (p. viii). This would explain why this model, along with the classic cube model (Morrill et al., 1974), is one of the two most cited models in the program development literature (Barr & Cuyjet, 1983, 1991; Barr & Keating, 1985; Cooper & Saunders, 2000; Cuyjet, 1996; Cuyjet & Wietz, 2009; Hurst & Jacobson, 1985; Saunders & Cooper, 2001; Styles, 1985). The cube is cited by seven of the newer models whereas this linear model is referred to five times. The linear model may be more practical due to the tangible steps that can be used by a practitioner. The student services program development linear model (Moore & Delworth, 1976) consists of the following steps:

1. Initiating the program
   a. Germinal idea
   b. Initial planning team
   c. Assessment
   d. Program suggestions
   e. Program selection
   f. Program's future
   g. Development of a full planning team
2. Planning program goals, objectives, delivery systems, and evaluations
   a. Program goals and behavior objectives
   b. Training
   c. Methods of intervention
   d. Program evaluation
   e. Research design
   f. Preparation for pilot test

3. Pilot program
   a. Program publicity
   b. Pilot program implementation
   c. Pilot program evaluation
   d. Program future
4. Program implementation (repeats pilot in full scale)
   a. Training procedures and materials
   b. Program evaluation
   c. Training of trainers
   d. Program offering
5. Program refinement
   a. Program maintenance
   b. Program spin-offs (Moore & Delworth, 1976)

Moore and Delworth (1976) conceded that due to the pressure to produce and enthusiasm to meet student demand and students' needs for services and programs, student affairs professionals have not always used systematic approaches in their development and implementation. The facts that despite programmatic success, failure, or outlived functionality on campus, there may be little understanding of how or why we create, modify, or eliminate programs. This may still be the case as a more recent article addressed the need to systematize a process for the adoption of programs based on best practices (Shutt et al., 2012) within the field. The 1976 training manual says the cube is used to introduce divergent thinking in the program suggestions phase. This linear model comprises five stages of initiating, planning, piloting, implementing, and refinement (Cuyjet, 1996; Moore & Delworth, 1976), although "five stages" is a bit deceptive due to the subsections and processes that occur within each stage.

Barr and Cuyjet Program Development Models

In 1983, Barr and Cuyjet outlined a five-step model that expressed another linear process similar to the previous linear model (Moore & Delworth, 1976). The model in this section, and the next two six-step models, represent general modifications of the same general approach to program development. To avoid redundancy these three models will be discussed in this same section. The initial five-step model was replaced 8 years later by the six-step model. The original five steps opened with assessment and addressed the needs of the student, environment, and resources similar to previous ecosystem models. Then they proceed to planning, implementation, postassessment, and administrative decision-making. Here assessment is more explicitly stated as the start of the program development process. The model closes the loop by addressing the process with postassessment at step 4. This five-step model includes many of the same components of the other models in this historical account. The sixth step was goal setting.

Five years later, Cuyjet (1996) offered further modifications—a modified six-step model. Concerning the changes, in the literature most authors tend to say the only change was the addition of a substep in the first step (i.e., past programming) where the history of programming on campus or in regard to the program in question is involved. Upon closer examination, there are six additional changes to the six-step model in this version. Within implementation, the substep of equipment is added. Five additional elements are added to postassessment (e.g., recognition and rewards, unexpected outcomes, programmers' reactions, ecological impact, and community building). Again, although the addition of these substeps seem appropriate and they should be included in a program development model, it seems as if their inclusion substantively alters the name of the fifth step from just postassessment to something different, perhaps program closeout, or merely postprogram phase, to be more inclusive of all the steps. To avoid redundancy, only the more complete model is presented here. The following is Barr and Cuyjey's (1991) six-step model for program development. The italics indicate the additional elements added (or altered) from the 1983 Barr and Cuyjet model.

1. Assessment
   a. *Current operations*
   b. *Student characteristics*
   c. *Needs*
   d. Institutional environment
   e. Resource assessment
2. *Goal setting*
   a. *Target population*
   b. *Desired outcomes*
   c. *Objectives*
3. Planning
   a. Planning team
   b. Approach
   c. Initial extent of program
   d. Training
   e. Timeline
   f. Budget

4. Implementation
    a. Responsibilities
    b. *Publicity*
    c. *Location*
    d. *Timing*
    e. Evaluation
5. Postassessment
    a. Analysis
    b. Fiscal evaluation
    c. Program modifications
6. Administrative decision-making
    a. Future plans

Hurst and Jacobson Program Development Model—Modified Cube

The only program development–specific book was published in 1985 (Barr & Keating, 1985). There a number of contributions to the student affairs program development literature, including a significant modification of the 1974 cube model. This model is referred to as the theoretical and conceptual foundations for program development (Hurst & Jacobson, 1985), or the "modified cube" for simplicity. The authors, including one of the original creators in 1974, kept the original three-dimensional shape and the three main intervention categories (i.e., target, purpose, and method). They continued to describe the model with the intervention vernacular, maintaining the original counseling approach to the development of programs within student services. They did change the order of the three main categories. Purpose is now priority 1, changing from priority 2. Target was swapped from priority 1 to priority 2. Method is still priority 3. The word *priority* is used here to delineate it from position, because graphically the positions of the three categories remain in the same physical location on each of the cube models. What has changed between the two models is the primary focus of program development on the purpose of the program and the target population becoming relative to the purpose.

The subelements of the modified cube also expanded with the purpose category, changing from three choices (i.e., remedial, preventative, and developmental) to seven. These categories are drawn from the seven dimensions of college student development formulated by Drum (1980): cognitive structures, aesthetic development, identity formation, physical health, moral reasoning, interpersonal relatedness, and social perspective (for a

Figure 2.3. Modified cube model.

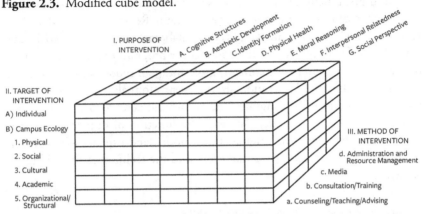

Note. This rendering adapted from Hurst and Jacobsen (1985).

more detailed explanation, see Hurst & Jacobsen, 1985, p. 202). The target category includes the individual (similar to the original cube) and then a second category of campus ecology. The method category seems to revert to more of a counseling paradigm in the modified cube than even articulated in the 1974 version. These new subcategories include (a) counseling/teaching/advising, (b) consultation/training, (c) media, and (d) administration and resource management. Although this model seems to be inclusive of the types of programs, who could participate, and how the modality of the program might be incorporated, it does not seem to be a functional model for the sake of planning and implementation. This conceptual model could be used as part of the germinal idea or brainstorming phase of the programming process. Figure 2.3 offers a visual representation of the modified cube model.

Barr-Keating Program Development Model

Barr and Keating (1985), the primary authors of the program development book, introduced another program development model. They incorporated the WICHE linear model and the 1974 cube to posit that three elements are needed for a successful program: context, goals, and a plan. The context of the program was described as greater society (American society implied), the institution and the environment of student services, and students. This section also noted the divisional and campus politics of programming. The goals included three overarching purposes of essential institutional services, teaching life management skills; and integrating the academic and cocurricular campus units. Finally, the plan consists of two distinct elements—the details needed to create and implement the program. Revisiting the 1985 Barr-Keating model, Cuyjet and Weitz (2009) elaborated on context, goals, and plan. This effectively adds another model for program development due to the graphic depiction of the context, goal, and plan model and the addition of substeps. This visual operationalization seems to make the original model more linear and provides tangible effects of what it takes to create and implement a program. This model also adds the function of implementation to the original elements. The original 1985 model, and explanation, said that the plan was two-fold in the actual event and the techniques of making it a reality.

Model for Future Program Development

The Barr and Keating (1985) book provided a third program development model for the field, known as the model for future program development posited by Marvalene Styles (1985). This model is depicted as a pyramid shape that incorporates five components: educational goals, student development theories, program development models (in existence by 1985), theory to practice, and the dimensions of psychological maturity. Every component includes an explanation about the need for both descriptive and prescriptive competencies. Hence, Style's chapter implied there is a need for the future of program development to incorporate these competencies. Starting the chapter summary with "Program development is the most critical function performed by student service professionals" (Barr & Keating, 1985, p. 207) illustrated that systematic purposeful planning connects the organizational (student services division) with institutional priorities.

Saunders and Cooper Program Development Model

Theory is the underpinning for the types of interventions planned and implemented through on-campus programming as described by the Saunders and Cooper (2001) program development model. This model is fitted more to the programming (e.g., event-like) aspects of program development and comprises two stages:

Planning

- Select a planning team
- Identify conditions and constraints
- Obtain agreement on pedagogies

- Review the skills and preferences of facilitators
- Create an agenda for program sessions
- Identify referral sources

Implementation
- Define responsibilities
- Make arrangements
- Establish the terms of collaboration
- Recognize that perfection is impossible
- Evaluate and redesign, if appropriate (p. 333)

The first stage of planning contains six subsections that are very similar to those outlined over the history of program development. Likewise, with the implementation stage this simplistic model combines the actual implementation process with some of the postprogrammatic functions of programming. From a quick overview of programming, this seems to encapsulate the "Plan-it/Do-it" approach to programming on campus. In addition to the programming considerations, Saunders and Cooper provide a succinct connection with college student development and learning theories as well.

Community-Building Program Model

Robert's (2003) community-building program model augmented the two-component approach of the Saunders and Cooper (2001) model while adding the component of outcomes. Roberts (2003, 2011) contributed the same model in the two subsequent editions of *Student Services: A Handbook for the Profession*. He drew a distinction between program development and community-building programming and connected them to contemporary leadership theories (Roberts, 2003). "The point of the community-building program model is not to compete with other program development and delivery models" (p. 544). He further explained that leadership theory had changed from a positional leader-centric model to a more inclusive team and transformational leadership theories that involve the leadership capacity of the whole; in short, it had become more synergistic and community level in approach. The community-building program model has the following main components (Roberts, 2011).

Planning
- Those interested in an idea join in the effort.
- Challenges and opportunities are identified.

- Multiple and related strategies are analyzed.
- Current capability and learning potential for planners are assessed.
- Resources are compiled from the network of extended supporters.
- Opportunities are prioritized based on the human, fiscal, and other material resources available.
- Responsibilities are distributed among the planners based on mutual agreement.

Implementation
- Initiators take responsibility for getting things started and engage others as they are available.
- Resources are confirmed, reservations made, and tasks distributed.
- Collaboration and mutual work is expected.
- Participants recognize that perfection is impossible and rework as necessary.
- Evaluate and refine.
- Reflect and survey the learning acquired by those involved.

Outcome
- Those involved see themselves as responsible for what happens.
- The capacity of the community and the leadership to deal with issues it confronts is enhanced.
- Problem-solving becomes a natural and sustainable part of the community environment.
- Community health and vitality are created and maintained (Roberts, 2011).

Other Models

The previous sections are about the models presented in the historical program development literature. The following models can be found in student affairs literature. Because they are program development models, they do share common elements, which we have been discussing, and these elements can also be mapped to the IMPD. Although other models exist and were included in the previous list, there is little evidence to show that these models were either influential on other models in history or that these models typically cite the predominant models listed in the student affairs literature. These models include the health and wellness model (Mosier, 1989), the student leadership program model (Roberts & Ullom, 1989), and the comprehensive leadership model (Haber, 2006), which was changed to the formal leadership model (Haber, 2011). The chapter on Styles's contribution (Barr & Keating, 1985) also included three models that could be interpreted for program development; however, they seemed more counseling-specific: the plan for intentional student development (Miller & Prince, 1976) and a schematic for change (Lewis & Lewis, 1974). The Drum and Figler (1973) outreach model mentioned by Styles was revised and incorporated into the Hurst and Jacobsen (1985) modified cube model.

Logic Models

In looking for a resource to teach and conduct the process of program development, we have seen some programs, programmers, and academics use logic models. A *logic model* is often described as a visual representation for how work will be conducted (Renger, 2002). The basic definition is "a systematic and visual way to present and share your understanding of relationships among the resources you have to operate your program, the activities you plan, and the changes or results you hope to achieve" (W.K. Kellogg Foundation, 2004, p. 1). The general diagram of such a model (see Figure 2.4) includes the two sections of planning and intention, which again takes us back to the original opening to this chapter—that changing something from a gamble to more of a sense of reality is purpose/planning and intent. A logic model has main sections of planned work and intended results. The subsections can be seen in the expanded logic model.

The logic model has primary applications in evaluation and program effectiveness. It has been used effectively as a program development model as well. "If . . . then" reasoning can lead the user through the steps (W.K. Kellogg Foundation, 2004). Although this is useful and seems natural, it approaches the development of a program through the process from a more static approach. This seems to be why the utility of logic models aligns more with the evaluation of an existing program versus the creation of a new program or concept from the fresh-new-idea phase of program definition. Although logic models can suffice for program development purposes, they

Figure 2.4. Simple logic model.

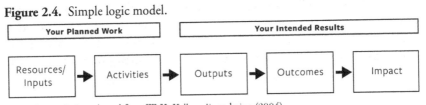

Note. This rendering adapted from W. K. Kellogg Foundation (2004).

Figure 2.5. Logic model expanded.

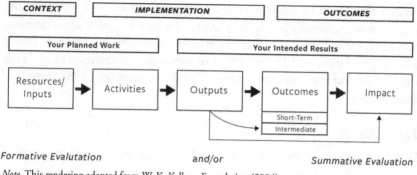

Note. This rendering adapted from W. K. Kellogg Foundation (2004).

seem to fall short of the holistic nature of the process. The move from planning your work to the intended results is good as far as it goes, but program development is a process of working from the inception of the idea through the analysis of the results and the closeout of the program budget, learning outcomes, and final assessment. Although a simple logic model covers the whole process in the planned work and the intended results, there is more going on under the surface. The expanded logic model (Figure 2.5) shows multiple layers adding context, evaluation, and ranges of outcomes. These models provide a rationale for why the program development model shows the main components, but various internal steps are actually happening along the way.

Connecting the Models

Figure 2.6 shows the history of program development models in the literature of student affairs in visual form. From this we can see there is a history and evidence that our program development ethos is tied to the aims, purposes, and precepts of campus curricular/cocurricular work. We can see the cube has the most connections to the latter models. The major players from a developmental and historical perspective seem to be the original cube model and the more linear student affairs model. This seems to support the idea that although we may see our programs as interventions per se, there is utility in the linear process of planning and development. This is also reiterated in the connections between the planned and intended results in a logic model.

Figure 2.6. Connecting the 45-year history of the models visually.

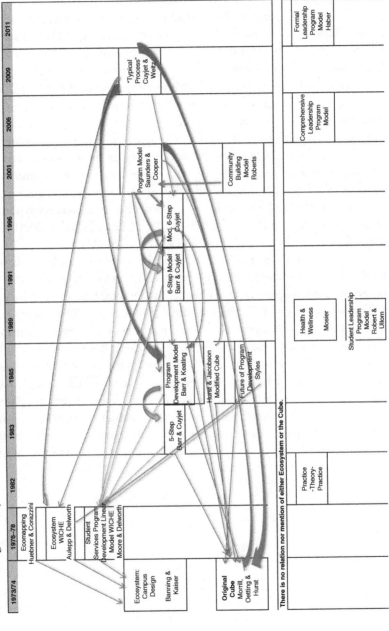

Conclusion

Program development is one of the key ways in which the student affairs professional contributes to the curriculum and overall mission of each institution (Barr & Keating, 1985; Cooper & Saunders, 2001; Saunders & Cooper, 2001; Styles, 1985). Programs, whether interpreted as department/functional areas or event-like activities (one time or within a series) are the translation of theory to practice (Saunders & Cooper, 2001; Styles, 1985). A model for program development offers definition, direction, and reflection for the service or event. This is true whether we function as the active programmer applying our expertise directly to the target populations (individual or student groups) or while functioning as the mentor programmer advising a student programmers group. Either/both are programming and program development. The model helps us plan to meet our goals to fulfill the needs of the student within the context of our campus ecosystems and institutional missions (Barr & Keating, 1985; Claar & Cuyjet, 2000; Cuyjet, 1996; Cooper & Saunders, 2000; Cuyjet & Weitz, 2009).

Over the course of the last 50 years, the history of student affairs on a local and national level shows that staff, faculty, and students have developed programs. This chapter has explained 21 models that have guided the student affairs community (ACE, 1937, 1949; Keeling et al., 2004; Keeling et al., 2006; Nuss, 2003; Roberts, 2003). You might ask if all program administrators and their teams use a model when developing a program. Schuh and Triponey (1993) wrote, "There is no best program development model, but we hold that those that do plan programs well normally use a program development model" (p. 430). We could not agree more and, therefore, our intent with the remaining chapters is to walk you through the process of program definition, planning, implementation, launch, monitoring, and reflection, to show how planning with purpose can be less of a gamble and more of a success.

3

WHY DEVELOP THIS PROGRAM?

After reading this chapter, you will be able to do the following:

1. Describe how various sources can indicate the need for a program
2. Identify sources of data to examine in establishing program need
3. Articulate how to determine if a program is not needed

Where do program ideas come from? Why develop this program? How do you know if a program is needed? How do you know if an existing program is no longer needed?

There are many possible sources for program ideas. Sometimes, the idea for a program comes from an external audience or stakeholder. For example, the parents' council may suggest implementing a program to help them support students' transition to college. Program ideas also can come from upper administration. For example, many campuses have initiated late night programming as part of their efforts to reduce student drinking (Patrick et al., 2010); your president may have heard of the success of such a program at a colleague's campus and suggests implementing it on your campus. Additionally, students can be the source of a program idea. For example, students may introduce the idea of implementing gender-inclusive housing on your campus (Chave, 2013).

National data or research might point out the existence of a problem nationally. Is that same issue a problem on your campus? For example, a national study found that food insecurity was prevalent among college students, with 48% of students surveyed reporting food insecurity in the past 30 days. The incidence of food insecurity was higher among African American students (57%) and first-generation students (56%) (Dubick et al., 2016).

What is the situation on your campus? Does your campus need a program that addresses food insecurity?

The institutional mission may indicate particular programming. Many campus mission statements refer to creating leaders; a tiered leadership development program might be indicated. Another common component in institutional mission statements is the intention to produce global citizens or graduates who can think globally; the creation of study abroad opportunities or a globally focused speaker series might be indicated. College mission statements that emphasize service to others support the creation of service-learning programs and alternative break service trips. Grounding programming in the institutional mission creates buy-in on the part of stakeholders and increases the likelihood of the program being effective for students (Chickering & Reisser, 1993).

> The basic point is that clear and consistent [institutional] objectives, stated in terms of desired outcomes for learning and personal development, are critically important in creating an educationally powerful institution. . . . Research evidence, dating back to Newcomb's (1943) detailed study of Bennington College, indicates that clear and consistent objectives make significant contributions to student development. . . . Clear and consistent objectives make for internally consistent policies, programs, and practices. (pp. 287–288)

It also is true that institutional mission may mitigate against the development of a program. For example, professionals at faith-based institutions may find that programs around sexual health and birth control do not fit with the mission or culture of the campus. It is important for program developers to understand the campus culture.

A program may sound like a good idea. It may be rooted in your mission. But is it needed? In either case, the next step is to conduct a needs assessment. The following section describes the needs assessment process, which is part of the program definition step of the program development model (see Figure 3.1).

Needs Assessment

As discussed previously, student affairs professionals often implement programs based on what they have learned from colleagues, what they have read, or the institutional mission, without determining if the program is needed (Upcraft & Schuh, 1996). Barr and Cuyjet (1991) recommended that the

Figure 3.1. Integrated model for program development—Program definition.

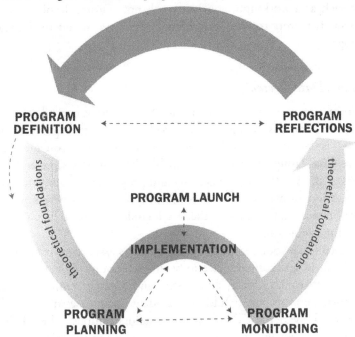

first step in program development should be assessment, including an assessment of student needs. Needs are often talked about in terms of the discrepancy between the current state and the desired state (Lee et al., 2007). According to Upcraft and Schuh (1996), a *needs assessment* "is the process of determining the presence or absence of the factors and conditions, resources, services, and learning opportunities that students need in order to meet their educational goals and objectives within the context of an institution's mission" (p. 128).

Kuh (1982) stressed that it is important to be mindful of the difference between student needs and student wants. Students may "want" a lazy river; what they need is a facility that supports fitness. This makes a well-designed needs assessment particularly important. Although it is not set within the context of higher education, *A Guide to Assessing Needs* (Watkins et al., 2012), published by the World Bank, provides an excellent overview of the entire needs assessment process.

A note about scale: The larger your program is, the more you should undertake a needs assessment. You certainly do not want to commit a significant amount of budget and staff time to the creation and implementation of a large program that is not needed. Conversely, for a very small program activity such as a workshop, you likely will not venture deeply into needs assessment. It is important to match your needs assessment to the scale of your program.

Document/Data Review

The information you require to determine if a program is needed may already exist on your campus. Therefore, an excellent place to begin your needs assessment is determining data that are already available to you and examining those data. Using these already available data can save time and money (Watkins et al., 2012) in your planning and program development. We will review a variety of places on campus where useful data may be housed, the information you might find, and the way it could be used to help determine the need for a program.

If available on your campus, a student affairs assessment office (or staff member) can be an excellent place to begin your search. The student affairs assessment office may create, administer, and analyze results of a variety of assessments on campus. In addition, student affairs assessment will likely be aware of the variety of data that exists across campus, where it is, and how to access it. Finally, student affairs assessment can provide assistance in developing your needs assessment and might even perform the needs assessment for you. As a first step, consult with student affairs assessment about the various ways they might be able to assist you in determining the need for your program.

The office of institutional research (IR) can be the source of a wealth of data that may assist you in determining whether a program is warranted. IR offices collect, analyze, and report institutional data. They also typically house data and reports from national studies in which your institution participates. Among the on-campus data that might typically be obtained from IR are data related to admissions, student credit hours, headcount, and retention rates. IR should have several years of such data, allowing you to track trends and identify changes in your student body. For example, a notable increase in first-generation students could suggest the development of a program to address first-generation students specifically, such as transition programs that impart "college knowledge" or a first-gen living-learning community. Lower retention rates among specific groups of students could suggest targeting those groups with retention programming, such as intrusive advising, supplemental instruction, or mentoring.

There are a number of national studies in which your institution might participate; the reports of the findings are likely to be housed within IR. We will highlight a few common national studies that might inform program development. You can check to see if your institution participates in any of these and also what other national assessments your institution participates in. The Higher Education Research Institute (HERI, n.d.) at UCLA administers a number of national surveys in which your institution might participate; among them is the Cooperative Institutional Research Program (CIRP) Freshman Survey, Your First College Year, and the College Senior Survey. The annual CIRP Freshman Survey has been administered nationally for over 50 years. Typically, the survey is conducted at the time of college entry (e.g., during orientation). It provides information about the incoming class, including their expectations for college; their high school experiences and behaviors; their perceptions of their knowledge, skills, and abilities; and their college admissions decisions and reasons for attending college. Among the high school experiences information gathered are participation in advanced placement courses, mental health, and civic engagement. In the knowledge, skills, and abilities section, students rate their strengths and weaknesses in a variety of areas. Expectations for college include such things as the likelihood they will participate in community service, study abroad, and undergraduate research. The Freshman Survey provides your institution's results and the aggregated results of comparison institutions. From this survey you can, for instance, gain insight into what your incoming students view as areas of weakness, suggesting the development of academic support programs in those areas, or what their level of interest is in various opportunities such as study abroad or community service.

HERI also conducts other, similar surveys, including Your First College Year (YFCY) and the College Senior Survey. YFCY is similar to the Freshman Survey and can be used as a follow-up. YFCY collects data at the end of students' first year of college and is focused on students' development during the first college year. Questions include activities students participated in, how they spent their time, satisfaction with elements of the college experience, and use of services. From YFCF you can learn how difficult your first-year students found it to manage their time effectively or to develop close friendships. Such information could indicate the need for programs around time management or additional community-building programs. The College Senior Survey is administered to seniors and explores their college experiences and how they may relate to a variety of outcomes. You can discover, for example, how seniors spent their time during a typical week, what your graduating seniors' plans are immediately postgraduation (full-time work, graduate/professional school, participate in a service organization such as the Peace Corps, etc.), and how satisfied seniors are with various aspects of their college experiences.

The National Survey of Student Engagement (NSSE; nsse.indiana .edu) collects information from participating 4-year institutions for first-year and senior students. The NSSE gathers information on students' participation in educationally purposeful activities and HIPs (Kuh, 2008): learning communities, service-learning, research with a faculty member, study abroad, internships, and culminating experiences (NSSE, 2013). Perhaps your institution's NSSE results indicate that your first-generation students are less likely to participate in HIPs, a national finding from NSSE in 2017 (NSSE, 2017). You may want to explore this finding further in additional needs assessment to determine what the reasons are for lower participation by first-generation students. There is a similar survey for 2-year institutions, the Community College Survey of Student Engagement (CCSSE; ccsse. org), that collects information about community college students' college experiences.

The Multi-Institutional Study of Leadership (MSL; leadershipstudy .net) collects data related to students' college experiences and educational and leadership outcomes. Among the college experiences explored by the MSL are mentoring, involvement in campus organizations, leadership development experiences, and academic-based experiences such as study abroad and first-year seminars. From the MSL you might learn that certain groups of students are much less likely to report being mentored or participating in leadership development. Such a finding could indicate a need to target further needs assessment in this area with these groups of students to explore the barriers they might be encountering.

Another source of useful data can be the housing and residence life department. Residence life departments often participate in annual or semiannual benchmarking to compare their performance to those of peer institutions (or aspirational peers). For example, Association of College and University Housing Officers-International (ACUHO-I) administers the Campus Housing Index that collects data annually on a variety of topics including residential programming, staffing, policies, facilities, and budget. Your campus's responses can be compared to those of other institutions (www.acuho-i.org/resources/cid/6105). Residence life also may collect data in a variety of areas including resident satisfaction, resident assistant performance, occupancy, damages, conduct incidents, and programs. Data from residence life may be particularly valuable if yours is a highly residential campus.

Many services and facilities on campus may collect data regarding the use of services (Upcraft & Schuh, 1996). These might include the campus recreation center, health services, counseling services, career services, student union, and tutoring. Such data should provide information on the number of students who use various services or facilities and the pattern of usage (time of day, time of the semester, etc.) as well as peak usage times. Demand demonstrated by utilization data can confirm the need for expanded facilities and/or operating hours and additional program offerings.

Many other offices may have relevant data. The specific offices will vary based on your project. Once you have explored the availability of data on your campus and what those data say, you can determine if you need to gather additional information. In some of the previous examples, for instance, we suggested that you might follow up certain findings with a more focused needs assessment on campus. In the following, we outline some approaches to conducting needs assessments.

Surveys

One of the most common methods to collect needs assessment data is surveys. Surveys enable you to collect information from large numbers of participants relatively quickly and efficiently. Surveys provide easily compiled and analyzed data. They can take the form of paper surveys or web-based surveys. Paper surveys can be useful when gathering information from captive audiences such as students at orientation. Paper surveys can also be administered very effectively via tabling, particularly if you are collecting information from students (Student Government Resource Center & College and University Food Bank Alliance, 2015). Web-based surveys have the advantage of requiring no additional data entry on your part, although some paper surveys can be scanned to compile the responses. Web-based surveys allow a variety of response formats (yes/no, scales, pick lists, etc.) and the use of "skip logic" (avoiding the need to say things such as "If you answered 'no' to question 16, please skip to question 37").

One problem with surveys, however, is that students on your campus may be "surveyed out" due to the number of requests for survey participation that they receive. If students on your campus are frequently asked to participate in surveys, schedule the administration of your survey so that it avoids some of the most heavily surveyed times. In addition, use your knowledge of the rhythm of the semester to guide your timing; your survey could get lost among the demands of the beginning of the academic year or finals week or heavily attended traditional campus events. You can read more about survey fatigue in chapter 8.

Survey questions must be worded carefully in order to gather information on needs rather than wants. In addition, as Henning and Roberts (2016) observed, "Because students may not be able to identify or know their needs, the questions must be carefully crafted based on the audience" (p. 70). In general, the creation of survey questions can be trickier than it appears. It is not uncommon to discover that a question you thought was clear was misinterpreted by many of your respondents, leaving you without the answer to your intended question. For example, one of us asked a survey question about types of on-campus housing, only to discover that many respondents did not understand the categories provided. One way to guard against this is to have a few people read and respond to your survey, preferably people who are similar to those to whom you intend to administer it. You can review their responses to see if they understood the questions in the way that you meant them. You also can discuss the experience of taking the survey with these pilot respondents to ask if they found any of the questions tricky or confusing. It is far better to realize that your questions are unclear before you administer the survey than to discover that they were unclear when you are trying to compile and interpret the results.

The details of survey design are too extensive to review here. There should be several people on your campus with survey design expertise; among them are the student affairs assessment office, office of institutional research, and faculty members who teach in areas of assessment and research. In addition, there are any number of good books specifically devoted to survey design that you can consult.

Interviews

Interviews give you the chance to gather more in-depth information than you can with a survey, although from fewer participants. Unlike with surveys, allow for the opportunity to clarify confusing questions. You also can ask follow-up questions that are prompted by the participant's responses. Interviews can provide deeper, richer stories than survey responses can give. The advice one of us received about assessment was to remember that some of the audience to whom you will be reporting your findings are "numbers people," whereas others will want to hear the stories; therefore, it is wise to collect both. Interviews can be an excellent way to collect those compelling stories.

When thinking about using interviews in your needs assessment, there are a number of considerations (Henning & Roberts, 2016). One of them is time. Interviews take time. Participants need to be recruited; interviews need to be scheduled based on their schedules and yours, as well as based on the availability of the space you will use for your interviews. In addition, you should be prepared for "no shows" and rescheduling of interviews, adding even more time to your timeline.

Additionally, need to consider your participants. You need to determine whom to interview and how to select them, as well as the optimal number of interviews to conduct. When considering selection of interview participants, avoid going automatically to the students who typically are consulted, such as student government leaders or student organization officers. Be aware of the possibility of hearing only some of the possible perspectives based on who is interviewed.

Logistics is another area to consider. In addition to the scheduling logistics mentioned previously, another logistical consideration is identifying an appropriate space to hold the interviews. Is the space quiet? Easily located? Another consideration is whether or not you will record the interviews. If so, make sure that your equipment is in working order—and make sure it is turned on! Too often professionals find, after the interview is over, that they have forgotten to start the recording. Recording the interviews will allow you to capture the interview more completely; however, participants may not want to be recorded. What is your plan if that is the case? Remember, written notes can be a game-saver when technology fails you (e.g., when you discover that your recorder did not record); however, note-taking can distract you from listening fully to the participants.

You will need an interview protocol to guide your interview. An interview protocol can ensure that you collect similar information from each interview participant. It will also help make sure that you cover everything you wanted to cover. Following an interview protocol also will help you stay aware of how much time you have used and how many more questions there are to go; thus, it can help you with the pacing of the interview.

Finally, once you have conducted your interviews, the recordings (if you recorded) will need to be transcribed. If you have ever transcribed an interview, you already know how time-consuming it is. If at all possible, we recommend that you have the recordings transcribed by someone who is skilled at it, which will take far less time. One of our colleagues likes to use Zoom for interviews because it will transcribe the interview. Although there are errors in that transcription, our colleague says she finds it less time-consuming to correct the errors than to transcribe the entire interview.

Analysis of the transcripts will require additional time. Remember, however, this is not intended to be a full-scale research project that requires a complicated coding system.

Focus Groups

A focus group is like an interview with a small group of people (often 5–12) (Watkins et al., 2012). A focus group allows you to hear from more people in a shorter time frame than interviewing them individually; more importantly, the focus group enables the participants to interact with one another, building on one another's responses. It is generally recommended to use an experienced focus group facilitator, rather than trying to do it yourself (Watkins et al., 2012). Saunders and Cooper (2009) observed, "There is an art and science to conducting effective focus groups, and one should consider the cost-effectiveness of hiring a trained moderator versus using a staff member with little or no experience in conducting focus groups" (p. 130). Many of the things to think about with focus groups are very similar to considerations for interviews.

As with interviews, thought needs to be given to participant selection. How will you select your participants? Similarity among participants along some relevant dimension (year in college, place of residence, etc.) is recommended (Garrison et al., 1999). As with interviews, however, be cognizant of the danger of hearing only some of the perspectives based on who is included.

The logistics of focus groups are quite similar to those of interviews. Think about timing, length, location, and recording. In addition, you will need to determine how many participants you want at each focus group; suggestions range from 4 to 6 to 10 to 12 (Cooper, 2009). Garrison et al. (1999) suggested that focus groups can take between 40 minutes and 3 hours, which is a very large range. Given students' typically busy schedules, 60 to 90 minutes may be a reasonable length. The appropriate length depends on the number of participants and the number of questions. In addition to recording, will someone also take written notes? Frequently, to encourage participation, food (snacks, lunch) is provided during the focus group. Will you offer other incentives for participation (Gansemer-Topf & Wohlgemuth, 2009)? Finally, how many focus groups will you run? The number will depend in part on how many different segments of the population you want to hear from and in part on practical logistical matters such as budget, the availability of space (often a precious commodity on campus), and the amount of time you have for this phase of needs assessment and program development.

Just like with an interview, a protocol for the focus group is important. The protocol can be particularly important if you are conducting multiple focus groups and especially if you are using multiple facilitators. The protocol will help ensure consistency across focus groups—which questions are asked, which follow-up probes are used, and so on. Schuh (2009) provided a strong example of a focus group protocol.

Unlike with interviews, there are things to consider having to do with group management. Members of the group may lead one another off on tangents. An important role of the facilitator is to guide the discussion back to the topic at hand; a skilled facilitator will know how to do that. In addition, it is not uncommon that some members of the group may be quiet and reluctant to speak up, whereas another one or more may attempt to dominate the conversation. Again, a skilled facilitator is needed to manage these dynamics. Watkins et al. (2012) cautioned that focus groups can have a tendency to fall into "groupthink." The facilitator should be aware of this and help guide the discussion away from "groupthink."

Finally, transcribing and analyzing are very similar to the considerations for interviews. Transcribing may be even more complex due to possible difficulties in distinguishing one participant from another.

Determining If a Program Is No Longer Needed

And what about existing programs that may not be needed?

> Often, we arrive at a new institution eager to begin our position and are immediately faced with a set of program initiatives that seem outdated, unnecessary, underused, or redundant. When we try to ascertain why programs are in place, we are met with responses such as "we have always done it that way," or "because Dr. X thought it would be a good idea," or "because we had a problem with that once," or "*The Chronicle* says it is a problem nationally, so we assumed it is a problem here." (Cooper & Saunders, 2000, p. 5)

Programs can consume large amounts of resources, including budget and staff time. If a program is no longer needed, those resources could be redirected more beneficially to programs that are needed, whether existing or new.

To begin, why do you think this program might not be needed? Declining or consistently low participation could be one indicator. Duplication with another similar program on campus could be another indicator. Information from program participants' evaluations (if they exist) may provide indications that the program is missing the mark or outdated. If you have inherited a number of programs with your new position, you could examine information of this kind to get a sense of which programs you might "go out of business" on.

For example, one of the authors once worked in a campus career center. The center had a program on the transition from student to professional that staff were very proud of and very invested in. Unfortunately, when the program was offered, attendance was sparse to nonexistent. Staff tried taking the workshop "on the road" to various academic buildings and residence halls. Attendance did not improve. Staff were frustrated because they liked the workshop and thought that the content was valuable; however, the program simply failed to draw students. Before we "went out of business" on the workshop, we recorded it so that it could be accessed online. Then we took it out of our program rotation so that we could use our resources to offer programs for which students perceived more of a need.

You may want to do a more extensive needs assessment that goes beyond these easy indicators. This may be particularly indicated if the program in question has deep roots in campus history or tradition or has been championed by influential individuals on campus. The "do we still need this?" needs assessment could employ the same types of approaches as those you would use in considering a new program.

Mountaintop State University Example

Mountaintop State University (MSU) is a public, comprehensive university located in the mountains of a largely rural western state. It enrolls approximately 12,000 students, the majority of whom are in-state students. On her way into the university one morning, the president of the university, Margaret Jackson, heard a story on NPR about food insecurity among college students. Jackson wondered whether food insecurity was a problem at MSU. She reached out to her vice president for student affairs, Anton Bruce, to see if he had any university-specific data on food insecurity. Bruce formed a small committee to look into the issue and make recommendations; he asked Brooke Turner, director of the campus union, to lead the committee. Through further reading, Turner and the committee learned more about the impact of hunger and food insecurity on students' success. Based on her interactions with MSU students, Turner suspected that food insecurity might be a problem on their campus; the committee's first challenge was how to determine its extent and whether there was a need to address it.

Because the needs assessment would ultimately determine whether there was a need for a campus food pantry (a very large program), the committee elected to conduct a rather extensive needs assessment. An examination of existing documents and reports revealed little helpful information beyond the number of Pell-eligible students enrolled at MSU. Information from the College and University Food Bank Alliance (CUFBA; cufba.org) led the committee to examples of existing assessments of food insecurity and hunger. The committee decided to conduct a large-scale survey, administered electronically, adapting these existing instruments. Doing the survey electronically meant that the data would be easily compiled, analyzed, and turned into helpful tables and graphs.

In addition, they decided to conduct focus groups with a number of different subpopulations of students, including students living off campus, students living in on-campus apartments, Pell-eligible students, and graduate students. Information from CUFBA was helpful in determining groupings of students to invite to focus groups. Given the diversity of the groups, the committee decided to schedule the focus groups on several different days and at several different times of day (breakfast, lunch, and dinner) and to serve a meal at each focus group. They worked with the director of student affairs assessment (SAA) to write the focus group protocol and SAA staff conducted the focus groups and transcribed each of them. Email invitations were sent to students who registered via a Google Form.

As the example of food insecurity at MSU points out, the program definition stage is important for making decisions for your community. This stage requires analysis of data on many levels to determine if a program is needed and contributes to the mission of the organization. This information not only establishes need but also offers context to establish goals, objectives, and outcomes for the program. These are critical components in the program definition stage, leading us to explore these concepts in the next chapter.

4

PROGRAM DEFINITION STAGE

Goals, Objectives, and Outcomes

"Would you tell me, please, which way I ought to go from here?"
"That depends a good deal on where you want to get to," said the Cat.
"I don't much care where—" said Alice.
"Then it doesn't matter which way you go," said the Cat.
"—so long as I get SOMEWHERE," Alice added as an explanation.
"Oh, you're sure to do that," said the Cat, "if you only walk long enough."

Alice's Adventures in Wonderland, Lewis Carroll (2014/1865, pp. 56–57)

After reading this chapter, you will be able to do the following:

1. Explain the differences between goals, objectives, and learning outcomes
2. Describe the roles of goals, objectives, and learning outcomes in the program development process
3. Create strong goals, objectives, and learning outcomes for your own programs

The Cheshire Cat's advice to Alice for navigating Wonderland applies to the process of program planning as well. If we don't much care about the specific outcome, almost any program will do. But if you don't know where you're going, how will you know when you get there? Goals, objectives, and learning outcomes help in program planning by articulating specifically what you intend to accomplish with this program and are part of the program definition stage in the IMPD (see Figure 4.1).

Figure 4.1. Integrated model for program development—Definition and planning.

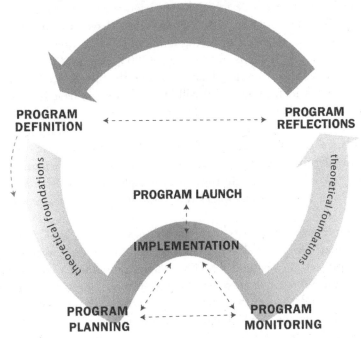

The terms *goals, objectives,* and *outcomes* are frequently confused and have been used interchangeably. However, they are in fact different, albeit related, concepts. This chapter presents the differences between these terms, the role of each in program development, and how to write strong goals, objectives, and learning outcomes. In addition, it will include helpful resources for writing goals, objectives, and learning outcomes.

A *goal* is the big picture of what you hope to accomplish. Goals are broad, abstract, and general. Goals often are focused on the long term. In the assessment of the need for the program (see chapter 3), gaps between the current situation and the desired situation were identified. The goal is a broad statement of the desired situation. Starting with what you intend to accomplish (the desired situation) and designing to reach that goal is "backward design" (Wiggins & McTighe, 2005). You work from your desired results to help articulate your goals, objectives, and outcomes, which in turn drive the content and the format of the program. In research, your question determines your design. You don't begin by saying, "I want to do a phenomenological study" or "I want to do structural equation modeling." Instead, you begin by stating clearly what it is that you want to know; that, in turn, determines your research design and your analyses. In the same way, your program is derived from what it is that you want to have happen, what is the change in students that you are trying to accomplish, or what it is that you want them to learn. Wiggins and McTighe (2005) described the three-stage approach to backward design. First, you identify the desired results (the goal). Next, you identify how you will know if students have learned what you intended for them to learn or changed in the way you intended (assessment); Wiggins and McTighe call this second stage "determin[ing] acceptable evidence" (p. 18). Finally, you design the learning experience (program) by considering the most appropriate way to get there (your program design). They suggested that "we might think of it as building a wise itinerary, using a map: Given a destination, what's the most effective and efficient route?" (p. 19).

A simple program or activity likely will have a single goal. A complex program may have several programs that fall under the larger complex umbrella project. An example of such a complex program is Welcome Week. For Welcome Week, such an overarching goal might be "to make first-year and transfer students feel that they are a part of the campus community." The overall Welcome Week program may be coordinated by the Division of Student Affairs, the Orientation Department, the Campus Activities Department, or some other unit. Typically, a large number of relatively independent programs and activities operate under the umbrella of Welcome Week, often designed and carried out by a number of different units on campus (Residence Life, Student Organizations, Dining Services, Career Development, Campus Recreation, etc.). For example, a complex program such as Welcome Week, which is an umbrella project with its own big goal, will likely have several goals in addition to its overarching goal. If the program has several different programs embedded within it, each of those smaller programs will have goals that will, when added together, equal the goal (or mission) of the program.

GOAL + GOAL + . . . + GOAL = OVERARCHING GOAL

Examples of program goals for programs included in Welcome Week might be "to encourage students new to campus to join campus clubs and organizations," "to make new students aware of campus resources," or "to facilitate new student and faculty interaction." Other (non–Welcome Week) examples of program goals might be "to improve the retention of first-generation students," "to increase the involvement of young alumni," or "to enhance student wellness." It is important to include only one desired change in each goal statement. In other words, do not write "to make students aware of resources and facilitate student/faculty interaction" as a single goal, but rather break them into two separate goals. This is because each will require its own activities for achievement and because it makes your assessment much clearer. You might have succeeded in making students aware of resources but not have achieved student/faculty interaction. In that case, did you meet your goal or not?

Objectives (also called *process objectives*) state what you, the program planner, are going to do to meet the goal. Objectives are narrow, specific, and precise. Objectives often are more short term than goals. Objectives focus on the implementation of the program, whereas *learning outcomes* focus on what the program participants will learn or how they will change. (Learning outcomes will be discussed separately in a later section.) It usually takes several objectives to meet a goal. Thus, the sum of all the program objectives will equal the program goal.

OBJECTIVE + OBJECTIVE + . . . + OBJECTIVE = GOAL

With more complex programs that have multiple goals embedded within them, each of those goals will have objectives.

Writing good objectives can be guided by the SMART criteria—specific, measurable, achievable, relevant, and time-bound (Doran, 1981):

- *Specific.* What exactly will you accomplish? The temptation is to make the objective too broad or too general.
- *Measurable.* What concrete criteria will you use to measure whether you have attained this objective?
- *Achievable.* Can you achieve this? Is it realistic?
- *Relevant.* Does this objective make sense within the context of the broader goal?
- *Time-bound.* By when will this happen?

Taken together, the SMART elements will provide a way to assess success. Doran (1981), who originated SMART objectives, noted that not every objective will contain all five criteria but that the closer the program planner comes to incorporating all five, the stronger the objectives would be.

Objectives will closely resemble your to-do list or checklist for the program. An objective might be, "By two months before the event, all space reservations will be made and confirmed" or "By the beginning of the academic year, the revised training manual will be printed for distribution at the first meeting of the year." Once you have made the objectives time-bound, they form a timeline. (See chapter 6 for more detailed information about objectives and timelines.) Writing objectives is relatively straightforward. The problem is when program planners write objectives when they mean to write learning outcomes.

Henning defined *outcomes* as "participant-centered, desired effects of a program service, or intervention" (as cited in Henning & Roberts, 2016, p. 85). Henning and Roberts (2016) likened outcomes to "destination postcards" (p. 86), specifying exactly where we are headed on our trip.

The ACPA/NASPA (2015) professional competencies addressed learning outcomes in several places. In the competency area of assessment, evaluation, and research (AER), foundational outcomes "design program and learning outcomes that are appropriately clear, specific, and measurable, that are informed by theoretical frameworks and that align with organizational outcomes, goals, and values" (p. 20), and intermediate outcomes "prioritize program and learning outcomes with organization goals and values" (p. 21). In the competency area of student learning and development (SLD), a foundational outcome is, "Construct learning outcomes for both daily practice as well as teaching and training activities" (p. 32), and an intermediate outcome is, "Create and assess learning objectives to evaluate progress toward fulfilling the mission of the department, the division, and the institution" (p. 32).

As with process objectives, learning outcomes add up to a learning goal.

LEARNING OUTCOME + . . . + LEARNING OUTCOME = LEARNING GOAL

Learning outcomes specify what students will learn or how they will change as a result of participating in the program. The common formula is SWBAT + action verb + specific learning. SWBAT is shorthand for "students will be able to." When writing learning outcomes for student programs, it is helpful to begin with the stem "As a result of [attending/participating in] [program], students will be able to" (SWBAT). In your needs assessment you identified the gap between the current state and the desired state. What is it that you want students to be able to do or how do you want them to be different as a result of participating in your program? Next, you need an action verb; students will be able to "what"?

To ensure that your objectives are measurable, it is helpful to turn to Bloom's (revised) taxonomy (Anderson et al., 2001; Krathwohl, 2002). Bloom's taxonomy provides a hierarchy of cognitive learning objectives from least to most complex (remember, understand, apply, analyze, evaluate, create) and sets of verbs pertaining to each level (recall, summarize, distinguish, critique, produce). See Figure 4.2 to see how Bloom's taxonomy supports writing objectives. (Visit https://cft.vanderbilt.edu/guides-sub-pages/blooms-taxonomy/#2001 for a helpful visual.)

Figure 4.2. Bloom's taxonomy supports writing objectives.

create	Develop new work
evaluate	Defend a stance
analyze	Determine the connections
apply	Interpret and utilize the information
understand	Identify and explain the ideas
remember	Commit concepts and facts

Note. Anderson et al. (2001). This figure represents Bloom's revised taxonomy.

Bloom's taxonomy will help you determine what level of complexity you are trying to reach (e.g., do you want students to recall knowledge, to apply knowledge, or to analyze information?)—for example, take suicide prevention training for resident assistants (RAs). Table 4.1 offers an example of using Bloom's taxonomy with this training.

Bloom's taxonomy also helps keep your learning outcomes specific and measurable, because it employs action verbs—things that students will be able to demonstrate. This is another place where program planners stumble. Program planners frequently state that students will be able to "appreciate" or "be aware." However, it is difficult to measure whether students "appreciate" or are "aware of" something. Even such things as "understand" or "know" can be more specifically stated and more readily evaluated if you use verbs drawn from the "understand" or "remember" level of the taxonomy. If you have a center for teaching or something similar (e.g., faculty development or instructional design) on your campus, staff there will be able to provide you with information on Bloom's taxonomy.

Not all learning is cognitive; you may have outcomes that are affective or physical/manual. If your objectives are not in the learning realm, Bloom's taxonomy still might provide you with a way to think about the possible hierarchy of verbs for your outcomes. It might be helpful to consult the lesser known taxonomies for the affective (Krathwohl et al., 1973) and psychomotor domains (Harrow, 1972). Once again, your campus's center for teaching or instructional design can be helpful to you in developing learning outcomes based on these lesser known taxonomies.

TABLE 4.1
Bloom's Taxonomy Categories Applied to Suicide Prevention

Bloom's Taxonomy Category	Definition	Example Using a Verb From the Taxonomy
Create	To produce new work	RAs will be able to *design* a suicide prevention bulletin board for their floor.
Evaluate	To justify a position or a decision	RAs will be able to *select* appropriate responses to statements made by a student in distress.
Analyze	To make connections between ideas	RAs will be able to *distinguish* signs of those in need of an immediate referral.
Apply	To use information	RAs will be able to *demonstrate* making a referral to counseling during the "Behind Closed Doors" part of RA training.
Understand	To explain facts and concepts	RAs will be able to *describe* the process of making a referral to counseling.
Remember	To recall basic facts	RAs will be able to *list* referral sources available to our university's students.

To make your learning outcome measurable, you should be able to quantify what you expect students to be able to do. For example, "After completing the Welcome Week scavenger hunt, students will be able to list the locations of at least six campus student services." The same SMART guidelines described previously can be used to write strong learning outcomes. Examine your outcomes to check whether they are realistic; for example, is six too high a number? Too low a number? In addition, examine your outcomes for their relevance to your goal. Does it make up a component that added to others will equal achievement of the goal? How does being able to list campus services fit into the overall goal? Finally, by when will students be able to do whatever is identified in your outcome? For example, "after completing [the program]" is a way of being time-bound; "two weeks after the completion of [the program]" is another. As you will see in chapter 8, this will be important for assessing the program.

Having your learning outcomes spelled out in such a clear and specific way, as in Table 4.2, enables you to be much clearer about the content that

TABLE 4.2
Using Bloom's Taxonomy and SMART for Learning Outcomes

Bloom's Taxonomy Category	Example Using a Verb From the Taxonomy	SMART-er Example
Create	RAs will be able to *design* a suicide prevention bulletin board for their floor.	*During the second month of the semester, all RAs* will be able to design a suicide prevention bulletin board for their floor.
Evaluate	RAs will be able to *select* appropriate responses to statements made by a student in distress.	RAs will be able to select appropriate responses to statements made by a student in distress *on a multiple-choice instrument distributed 3 weeks following RA training with at least 75% accuracy.*
Analyze	RAs will be able to *distinguish* signs of those in need of an immediate referral.	RAs will be able to distinguish signs of those in need of an immediate referral, *during the role play portion of suicide prevention training.*
Apply	RAs will be able to *demonstrate* making a referral to counseling.	*Seventy-five percent of RAs* will be able to demonstrate successfully making a referral to counseling *during the "Behind Closed Doors" part of RA training.*
Understand	RAs will be able to *describe* the process of making a referral to counseling.	*At the end of RA training, all RAs* will be able to describe the process of making a referral to counseling *during a one-on-one meeting with their supervisors.*
Remember	RAs will be able to *list* referral sources available to our university's students.	*At the end of the RA training session on mental health and campus resources, all RAs* will be able to list *at least three on-campus* referral sources available to our university's students.

you will include in your design and delivery of the program (Brown, 2019; Henning & Roberts, 2016). If you want students to be able to list the locations of at least six campus resources, you will need to include the location of campus resources in your program. If you want RAs to demonstrate their skill at making a referral during "Behind Closed Doors," you will need to teach that skill during training and build that scenario into the program. More about program design will be seen in chapters 6 and 7.

Once you have written your learning outcomes, we recommend that you review them to determine if together they fully address your goals for student learning. As Brown (2019) explained:

> Developing goals and outcomes is not a top-down-only process, but a reciprocal one. Each successive stage should inform and be informed by the other. . . . At each successive stage return to earlier points in the process to ensure that objectives align and that all concepts are accounted for. (p. 47)

We have found that, although the writing of learning outcomes seems straightforward, professionals frequently struggle with the task. The most common pitfalls we see are writing process objectives (which focus on what the program coordinator and staff will do) when the focus should be writing learning outcomes (what the students will learn or how the students will change) and failing to make learning outcomes measurable (usually because the verb selected is not measurable, as in *appreciate*) or specific. Reviewing your learning outcomes carefully to make sure that they really are learning outcomes and not objectives and to make sure that they are measurable and specific (use the SMART criteria) can help to ensure that your learning outcomes are strong. And, as with many things, practice helps. Try the exercise of taking an existing program. Does it already have learning outcomes specified? If so, try to make them stronger using Bloom's taxonomy and SMART criteria. If learning objectives are not already specified for the program, try writing some. Strive to make them as SMART as possible. Then, it is helpful to have someone who is experienced at writing learning outcomes review what you have written and provide constructive feedback on how your learning outcomes could be improved.

When SMART objectives and learning outcomes are developed that equal a well-defined goal, we, unlike Alice, are not only specifying where we want to go but also answering our own question of how to get there. We are further setting the stage to evaluate whether or not we have arrived at our intended destination and how successful the trip was.

Mountaintop State University Example

Let's return to MSU's desire to address food insecurity. They conducted a needs assessment that indicated a concerning level of food insecurity among their students (see chapter 3). The needs assessment confirmed the need to address food insecurity at MSU.

The committee's overarching broad goal is to reduce food insecurity among MSU students. Within their overarching goal, they have developed four goals (each still broad):

1. Raise awareness on campus of food insecurity and its impacts
2. Raise awareness of available resources for food insecure students
3. Establish a campus food pantry
4. Provide education to students about food shopping and nutrition

Notice that all of these goals focus on what the program planners intend to do, not on the outcomes for students. Objectives and learning outcomes where appropriate (probably goals 1, 2, and 4) need to be developed. This task most likely will fall to the MSU staff members who are chosen to coordinate this program (because it is not an existing program and, therefore, in no one's job description); this might include some of those on the committee. Other members of the committee may take more of a supporter role. Some might help to form the core of an advisory committee.

Some objectives for goal 3 might look like the following:

Goal: Establish a campus food pantry

1. Consult with risk management (CUFBA, 2015)
2. Identify campus location for the food pantry (CUFBA, 2015)
3. Develop an operations manual

And so on through staffing, supervision, solicitation of donations, and other logistical concerns. In each case, the objectives can be made more time-bound by adding a deadline to each, which will enable them to add it to their timeline (see chapter 6). The SMART guidelines will help the MSU Food Insecurity committee make objectives more specific.

For goal 1, objectives will address what program planners and staff will do.

1. The Mountaintop Food Bank steering committee will conduct a Food Insecurity Awareness media campaign during the first month of the semester.

Goal 1 also needs learning outcomes. A first try at this might look like the following:

Goal: Raise awareness of food insecurity on campus

1. Students, faculty, and staff will be able to describe the extent of food insecurity at MSU.
2. Students, faculty, and staff will be able to list the impacts that food insecurity has on student success.

Notice that the learning outcomes now indicate the content needed to achieve the goal as well as the audiences for the program. Again, these learning outcomes can be made much more specific by applying the SMART framework. For example:

1. *After the Food Insecurity Awareness media campaign, 85% of* students, faculty, and staff will be able to *state accurately what percentage of MSU students experienced food insecurity during the past month.*

This restatement of the learning outcome is more specific, measurable (exactly what they will be asked to do is indicated), achievable (a realistic percentage of people is stated), and time-bound (after the media campaign).

The MSU program coordinators will develop objectives and learning outcomes for each goal, taking care to make them as SMART as possible. Throughout the process, they will check to make sure that the learning outcomes, objectives, and goals are aligned. With another element of the program definition stage accomplished, it is time to think about resources. The next chapter will focus on budget and budgeting in the program definition stage of the IMPD.

5

PROGRAM DEFINITION AND PLANNING STAGES

Budget Essentials

After reading this chapter, you will be able to do the following:

1. Define *budget*
2. Articulate the importance of the budget in the program definition stage of the IMPD
3. Develop a budget for a new program that communicates required resources
4. Understand techniques that promote fiscal accountability

The following scenario identifies a key element within the IMPD: the budget. This chapter will focus on many significant elements of a budget and how it fits into the program definition and the program planning stages of the IMPD (see Figure 5.1).

It is important to define *budget* and what items are addressed in a budget. Next, the focus is on developing a budget that accommodates the needs of the program. Once the budget is developed, the funding process will be explored to understand the fiscal resources to meet program needs. The chapter concludes by addressing financial accountability to promote future fiscal responsibility. Let's begin with the following scenario:

> The Academic Advising Center reported to the associate vice president (AVP) of academic affairs. I met with him every 2 weeks to discuss the productivity of all units in my portfolio. These meetings usually included brainstorming ideas that addressed the mission of the institution. Programs

that the Academic Advising Center had been successful with over a 3-year period were a major Expo (Fair), a Meet Your Adviser Social, and a campus conference for academic advisers. Even though each event took time, an operating budget was developed and funded and I was able to equally distribute the workload over the staff without reducing individual student contact time or staff development time. At today's meeting, the AVP praised all these successful events, then he suggested that the Academic Advising Center should also add a Transfer Center and a Student Success Center. I appreciated his acknowledgment of the success the team had achieved with these programs that happened once a year for students and advisers on a small operating budget. Then I explained that these are annual events, whereas his new ideas are programs that serve students daily and require staff, space, and an operating budget. The scale of magnitude between an annual program and a program that engages students every day adds complexity to the process, including the budget. I welcomed the opportunity to review the literature, develop an implementation plan with a budget, and identify possible locations for these programs. Upon exiting the meeting, I stopped to make a few notes from our conversation, including "scale of magnitude" because it really nuanced the difference between earlier assignments of annual events and the current request for programs that would engage students daily.

Figure 5.1. Integrated model for program development—Definition and planning.

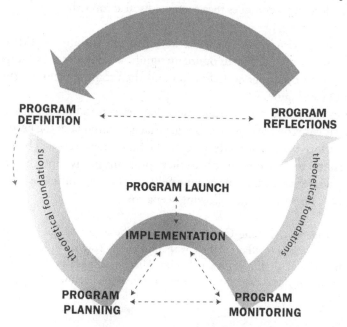

Budget—What and Why?

The word *budget*, when used as a noun, is a fiscal plan to guide an activity, program, department, or organization (Barr, 2002). Budgets exist on the institutional level in higher education for many important reasons. First, the budget identifies income streams for the organization to establish how much money is available. Second, a budget allocates resources between what is needed (essential) and what is wanted (optional) throughout the organization. Third, a budget offers an opportunity to motivate actions that prudently spend campus dollars while achieving the mission. Fourth, the budget can be a form of fiscal control. Some institutions use a central control system that reviews all expenditures, whereas others will follow a decentralized model that places budget authority for expenditures at the unit or program level. Other campuses will use a hybrid that combines elements of both. Finally, the budget communicates publicly the priorities for the organization. It clearly addresses continual commitments, such as salaries and utilities, but also defines the allocations of resources to initiatives that speak to strategic goals and the campus mission (Maddox, 1999). Budgeting at the organizational level is a key skill to understand, as is an awareness of resources to support your growth. This chapter will focus on defining the concept of budget and explaining the budgeting process for program development.

For the purpose of this book, the budget will be an important tool for building an idea into a proposed program, whether a single event (e.g., major fair) or a service available daily (e.g., student success center). A budget request will clearly communicate what resources are needed to accomplish the program's goal and objectives. The program coordinator builds a budget through the budgeting process and secures resources as part of the program definition stage. The program planning, implementing, and launching stages might identify needs that require additional resources, which the program coordinator would pursue through a supplement request process or document for future budget proposals. Finally, during the program reflection stage, the program coordinator and planning team should reflect on the budget to edit for future iterations of the program. Because developing a budget for an activity or program is a key skill for student affairs leaders, this chapter will begin by exploring budget development for a new program and then transition to broader topics around a unit budget.

Budgeting—A Subprocess in Program Development

Budgeting has been defined as the "process of expressing quantified resource requirements (amount of capital, amount of material, number of people) into time-phased goals and milestones" (BusinessDictionary, n.d.). Similar to an organization or a department, a program requires a clear budget, which is developed through the budgeting process. This process requires the program coordinator to consider some key questions:

- Who is sponsoring and involved in budgeting for the program?
- How does this program complement the mission of the department and/or organization?
- What resources are needed to deliver the program?

Let's explore each question.

It is important for a new program to have a sponsor. A sponsor is a steward or responsible party for the program. This sponsor might be a department, unit, division, or a mix within the campus organization. This assignment might emerge because a vice president of student affairs has asked a unit to explore solutions for a campus issue or a department has identified a solution to a problem or issue due to interaction with students. It is not uncommon in today's higher education environment for multiple departments to see an issue impacting students and decide to collaborate on the solution. Thus, the budgeting process should include all the parties involved in developing and delivering the program, with one party (sponsor) accepting responsibility for overseeing the program and the budget. The assignment of program coordinator or program administrator from the sponsoring department is not to exclude others but to ensure that a steward is responsible for leading the project through all stages of the IMPD to achieve the launch stage.

The group of people involved in the budgeting process must have a clear understanding of the purpose for the program and open the budget proposal with the rationale for the program. The rationale should be concise and connect the program to departmental and/or institutional mission and strategic goals. The authors of this book suggest starting the budgeting process conversation with this clearly articulated to understand scope and to avoid confusion on needs. Schloss and Cragg (2013) reminded administrators that "money follows mission" (p. 102). Thus, a strong budget proposal clearly connects the goals of the program to the institutional mission.

Next, the members should brainstorm the resources needed to deliver the program goals. Personnel, space, technology, and operating expenses are broad categories of needs to discuss as a group. Let's define and describe each of these categories with an example that focuses on a food pantry.

- *Personnel.* This category refers to the staff needed to achieve the goal of the program. It is important to consult with the human resources/ human capital department to understand the financial details of staff and faculty classifications as well as policies for benefits. For example, if the program requires a new staff member for daily management of the food pantry, the human resources department explains potential staff classifications that include salary range. Also, it is common for a budget with a staff request to include salary and estimated benefits, which is often a set percentage of total salary.
- *Space/Facilities.* This category refers to permanent physical space that the program might need for operation. If the program needs space, it is important to offer details such as square footage, potential locations to serve population, and services such as network connectivity, power, audio-visual systems, air conditioning, or natural light.
- *Technology.* This item includes hardware and software that are needed for the program tasks. It includes computers, printers, and accounting software. The food pantry will need to maintain an inventory of food received and distributed as well as utilization by students.
- *Capital Budget.* This budget item refers to items (of a certain dollar amount) that are purchased for the program and are used over multiple years as well as physical space (e.g., buildings). The example of the food pantry might include the purchase of commercial refrigerators and freezers.
- *Operating Expenses.* This item addresses the items needed for daily operation to achieve the mission that a department is responsible for at the institution. Common expenses include (but are not limited to) office supplies, printer maintenance contracts, travel costs, food, promotional items, and speaker honorariums. An example of one item for the food pantry is a weekly rental of a university vehicle to transport food from the local food bank to campus. It is important to note that this category requires considerable thought as the initial budget is developed for a new program.

As the program coordinator prepares for the meeting of collaborators, creating and sharing a worksheet that outlines the broad categories shared previously (or adjusted for specific campus budget categories) will stimulate the group conversation. Additionally, it offers a document to record program needs with costs. The program coordinator guides the budget dialogue and records the details, including estimated costs, potential vendors, and impacts due to institutional policy. It is paramount to maintain detailed notes for this meeting as well as all meetings. This documents your process. It is also advised to share these notes with other collaborators and partners for accuracy and transparency.

This meeting is also an opportunity to discuss resource contributions from partners. Why? First, some of the needs of the program might overlap with resources in another department. For example, a food pantry might need space for storage of canned goods. Another department might have this space due to a recent institutional decision to not print college catalogs, so a large closet for storage is available and close to the food pantry location. Second, the repurposing and sharing of institutional resources for new endeavors demonstrates buy-in for the new program within the campus community as well as prudent fiscal management at the department level. This opportunity to brainstorm with invested colleagues in the budgeting process provides the program coordinator with a thoughtful list of needs, estimated costs, and cost-sharing opportunities. Partnerships and collaboration pay dividends when starting new programs.

Upon completing this meeting, the program coordinator has sufficient information to develop a budget for future consideration. An important step toward a draft budget is to add numeric amounts to each item and the source or vendor. It is important to review institutional policies concerning sourcing of items in the budget. To accomplish this task, it is recommended that the program coordinator contact the departmental budget manager or assigned staff member for budget issues to explore these points. This individual will understand the nuances of the budget for the department and the broader financial landscape of the institution and will guide the program coordinator through budget policies as well as expectations for communicating the budget proposal in the department as well as campus-wide budget presentations. Potential questions for the program coordinator to ask the budget manager include the following:

- What is the process for reviewing this budget for approval?
- What are institutional policies concerning purchasing from noncampus sources and vendors?
- How should the budget be organized for review by various levels of the budget allocation committee for approval?
- How should the budget forecast future needs?

These questions direct the program coordinator on next steps in the budgeting process for their specific institution. It clarifies how resources are allocated to meet fiscal needs for the new venture. Let's explore the budget allocation process and the actual budget document.

Budget for an Activity

As you think about programming, it is important to identify the size and extent of the program, also known as magnitude. Is it a one-time activity, an annual event, or a new service with which students will engage every day? The answer to this question will help you establish the type of budget that you need to develop. Table 5.1 offers guidance on the budget based on the type of program and how often it occurs.

Now that you have identified the program type by the temporal characteristic, it is paramount to develop the appropriate budget. This chapter will explain a program budget starting with a single activity such as a major fair and then explore the budget process further with budget examples for a food pantry. Both examples offer depth and breadth for a program budget and the budgeting process.

Budget for a New Activity Offered Once or Once a Year—A Major Fair

As the opening scenario explains, it is quite common for new ideas to be a part of conversations in higher education. Regardless of whether the conversation is among colleagues, with students, or in a regular meeting with leadership, there are always conversations about opportunities to impact the student experience through programming.

These conversations often focus on a single activity that might occur once or more than once over a long period of time. In this case, the office or service area assuming ownership (or sponsorship) of the activity will be

TABLE 5.1

Budget Based on Type of Program and How Often It Occurs

Type of Program	How Often Does It Occur? (Temporal Characteristic)	Budget
Activity	One time	Operating expenses
Event	More than once but not every day (e.g., quarterly, annually, once a term)	Operating expenses in a department/unit budget
Multiple activities for a service or center	Continually in operation throughout the year	Personnel, facilities, start-up budget, annual allocation with operating expenses

responsible for the program plan, including the budget. In these cases, the budget is usually an operating budget. Due to the one time appearance of the activity, personnel costs are absorbed by the service or unit that has assumed ownership. If there is need for space or a facility and this need is not provided without cost, rental fees will be built into the operating budget. It is clear that an activity needs an operating budget.

The operating budget really focuses on resources needed to accomplish the program goal. It is important to create a list of all possible needs. There are many ways to begin this budget process to identify specifically what the program will need. Suggestions for starting the budget include the following:

- Brainstorm the cost of various items/services needed for this activity. Document for future use. (This strategy was covered earlier in this chapter.)
- Invite colleagues and students to review your draft of a budget items. Ask for feedback on what is missing.
- Have other institutions offered this activity? If so, is the budget available to review?
- Attend this event at another institution, inventory the event, and build a budget that meets the needs at your institution.

These activities as well as others that you develop begin the budget process. Table 5.2 offers a list of possible items needed for an operating budget for a major fair.

There are many items included in an operational budget. The success of your event depends on being as precise as possible to identify what you need. The next step is finding sources for these items as well as the cost. Many campuses have a purchasing unit that will offer information on credible vendors for pricing. An annual event expands skills for developing an operating budget. A daily service, such as a food pantry, is an opportunity to explore additional components of the budgeting process.

The Budgeting Process—A Food Pantry Serving Students Daily

Every campus will have a budgeting process or cycle. As stated previously, check with the budget manager or budget office to understand the process for the campus. Based on our experiences with developing budgets for new programs on our campuses, we share some key points to consider as you prepare your budget submission. A food pantry that is open continuously through the academic year will provide an example throughout this section.

TABLE 5.2
Items in an Operating Budget

Item	What You Need to Consider
Space for the activity	Does your campus rent space? If so, which spaces will meet your needs?
Food	Does the event offer refreshments or meals? Can you estimate the number of people being fed?
Sustainability costs	Will your event be a green event? If so, what costs might you incur such as recycle containers and dishes, cups, and silverware that need to be collected and washed?
Prizes	Is there a need to offer prizes? Maybe the event will have a competition that will be judged for a prize?
Decoration	Does the event require a specific type of decoration? Balloons, confetti, a giant bouncy castle are just a few of the options that people use.
Marketing	How will you inform the campus about your event? Who is the event targeted to and how do they receive information? Do you need to advertise on radio or TV? Do you need banners to hang around campus?
Entertainment	Does your event need to have entertainment such as a keynote speaker or chamber music? If so, think about options. Do you need a sound system or speakers?
Rental items	Do you need tables, chairs, or tents? How many?
Technology	Is there software or hardware that you need to rent or purchase?

First, it is important to understand the budget allocation process on your campus. Some key questions to ask are the following:

- What is involved in the budget process, especially resource allocation for the department and the entire campus?
- Who are various staff involved in the budget process?
- What are the department and campus timelines for receiving and reviewing new budget requests?

From asking these questions, the program coordinator will have an understanding of key details as well as a holistic process that moves revenue to campus departments as budget allocations to support a variety of activities, including new programs.

Second, the process that the program coordinator will follow to request a budget allocation will depend on the location of the program within the organization, how much the program costs to deliver, and how often it will be delivered to students. Here are some possible scenarios to consider. Many programs are assigned to a department or division. If this happens, it is important to know how the budgets are established and funded to meet program needs in the department or division. This includes a meeting with a department director or an assistant vice president for the division. Based on the level of financial need to implement this program, the program coordinator might not need to take the request further. A decision is made to fund or not fund. If the decision is to fund, the department or division will clarify what is required for submission and when to submit this request. For example, if a staff member wants to support students during final exam periods by giving away protein bars, the cost might be something that the current department or division budget can absorb without further review.

But some new programs require substantial financial resources for development and implementation. Thus, the department or division head might recommend the budget for this program be reviewed against other requests for new programs in the upcoming year. Most campuses will have a timeline for the annual budget review and allocation process. The director, division head, or budget director will explain the process and what the program coordinator needs to prepare on behalf of the program. Pay close attention to institutional dates, deadlines, and templates. Yes, details matter for the budget process as well as the programming process. It is highly recommended to have someone, preferably familiar with the process, review the submission documents. It is important to remember that the process outlined here will focus on campus resources that emerge from tuition (public and private institutions) and legislative funds (public institutions). There are other sources of revenue to launch a program and maintain it either partially or fully. This will be explained later in this chapter.

Third, identify the specific components required for the budget proposal by the department and/or campus. Break each component of the budget into an individual section that offers the reviewer ease in understanding the program and financial needs. The budget request document often includes a concise statement with goals and a comprehensive budget with exact costs including the operating budget, anticipated activities for accountability, and an appendix. The document includes page numbers and each of these sections is labeled for quick reference. Let's explore each section.

The concise statement opens the budget. It explains the issue, problem, or opportunity the program will address, the impact the program will have on the campus community, and the connection to the mission. This statement is brief and compelling with appropriate data that provide evidence to

Figure 5.2. Opening statement for a budget.

The food pantry addresses the issue of food insecurity among students and their dependents. Local and national data indicate that one in five students experience food insecurity while in college. At this institution, 65% of the students are Pell-eligible and 52% indicate supporting one or more dependent children under the age of 12 while enrolled in college. The closest food pantry to our campus is a 15-mile drive. A recent survey of students who withdrew during the term indicated that 42% needed to work more to provide basic necessities such as food for their children. Thus, they had to reduce their course load and delay time to graduation. (See Appendix for complete data.)

The goal of the proposed on-campus food pantry is to serve 100 students a week with 500 different students using the pantry over the fall and spring terms. The food pantry will offer our students quick access to a variety of fresh, frozen, and canned foods. It offers a key resource for students to nourish themselves and their children without having to seek additional employment at the cost of their degree completion, which addresses University X Strategic Goal #4.

support funding of the program. These data references are sparse but powerful, with comprehensive data available in an appendix. The concise statement should be clear on program goals that complement the issue. Figure 5.2 offers an example of the opening statement.

The next section of the budget proposal will present the budget, with needs expressed as specific items as well as the cost for each item. In this section, clearly identified items needed for the program are presented, including operating budget items communicated previously. A key component of this section is estimating the cost of each item over the period of time the budget is in use, which is usually 1 year. Thus, the program coordinator must engage their forecasting skills to produce a budget that will communicate the annual need. If the institution has a spreadsheet or template for the budget, make sure to use it. Those individuals tasked with reviewing budgets at the department or institutional level know these documents. Thus, they quickly focus on the goals and financial needs without confusion. If there is no template, Table 5.3 offers an example that one of the authors has used for creating budget requests for programs that serve students. Also, Excel offers a number of templates that might meet specific needs.

The following are a few additional thoughts on the actual budget that describes the needed resources to deliver this program. As Table 5.3 indicates, the budget addresses anything that the program will need financial resources to pay for as you begin and then sustain the program. Thus, it is important to identify one-time costs that allow the program to start as well as ongoing needs for sustaining the initiative. It is also recommended in the budget presentation to divide these financial needs for clarity between the annual costs for the program and the "start-up" costs. Also, this is an opportunity to identify the financial contributions from campus and community

TABLE 5.3
Tool for Creating a Budget

Budget Item	Description	Vendor	Cost	One-time (O) Or Continual (C)	Annual Cost for 2019–2020
Refrigerator	Commercial refrigerator to maintain dairy products	Used from Kroger	$750	O	$750
Signage—Open and close/specials	Sandwich board (5) to advertise outside pantry as well as other high-traffic areas of campus	Build A Sign.com	$57/each	O	$285
Maintenance contract for refrigerator and freezer	A maintenance agreement for annual maintenance or unexpected repair	Appliance Repair, Inc.	$500	C	$500
Space for food pantry	12 × 12 space needed for the food pantry; needs to have multiple power outlets/voltage for refrigerator/freezers	Union	$150/week; 52 weeks in a year	C	Partner union administration providing for this item in budget cycle

partners. This acknowledgment of collaboration signals financial teamwork in addressing the needs of students and creates community among campus partners. For example, in Table 5.3 you will see that the student union is supplying the space for the food pantry, which eliminates a cost for 2019–2020, but an estimate is provided anyway due to possible changes in the future.

Another key point about budget requests is the actual numbers. Basically, have the sums been added on all items over the 12-month cycle of the budget to represent the actual amount needed to deliver this program? Check the math and don't hesitate to ask colleagues to review the budget, including the actual arithmetic. This point can't be stressed enough, as budgets for higher education organizations have limited revenues to distribute through the campus budget process. Additionally there is competition among many departments for these finite resources (Barr, 2002). Thus, a budget allocation for the program must accurately cover the entire year.

The next section in your budget proposal briefly addresses accountability measures. First, it is important to explain the processes in place that address assessment of program goals for students' need, satisfaction, and learning. Needs assessment is covered in chapter 3 and outcomes assessment strategies are covered in chapter 8. Based on this later chapter, you should write a brief review of anticipated key tools and indicators for measuring program success. Second, it is strategic to have a plan for fiscal accountability. This plan should identify who administers the budget and reconciles the accounts, as well as how often the budget is reviewed with respect to the 12-month forecast (e.g., monthly, quarterly, etc.). A great tool for tracking expenses is a monthly review that is shared through a spreadsheet. This monthly review captures expenditures over the entire year as allocations are spent. A component for developing this review is the collection of receipts by staff for all expenditures. The program coordinator needs to reinforce this practice with staff and clearly articulate who is the central collection point for the receipts. It is common to organize monthly review based on institutional line items or budget fields. The budget manager is a good resource for understanding budget line items or budget fields. Some common budget fields are salary, benefits, travel, food, memberships, office supplies, and annual maintenance contracts. These are units of budget analysis that fit into budget categories that were addressed earlier in the chapter (personnel, space/facilities, technology, capital budget, and operating expenses). Third, offer some comments on sustainability of this program over a period of time. By addressing sustainability, the budget office will be aware of whether the program is a one-time request or an ongoing request until there is not a student need. One of the authors found that attention to accountability for the budget created trust and respect with many campus partners and produced additional opportunities for collaboration in developing new programs.

A final section in the budget proposal is an appendix. As evidence that supports implementation of this program is extensive, you can add various tables with data and pertinent literature from journals and newspapers in this section. It offers further evidence for the budget allocation team to review and confirms that the program coordinator did their homework in identifying the need for developing this program. The following documents are suggested as appropriate parts of an appendix section:

- Institutional data that support need (e.g., Pell Grant statistics, completion data, or enrollment data)
- State data that identify an issue
- Articles from scholarly journals
- Articles from *The Chronicle of Higher Education*

The budget proposal is a significant document for the IMPD. It is part of the program definition stage and will impact the program planning stage as the program emerges. It is a financial plan for the program and requires detail and precision to communicate the goal of the program, how the resources accomplish the goal, and what specifically is required to deliver this new opportunity. The process and documents explained previously address the allocation of revenue received from tuition and legislative allocations, but there are a few other sources to consider as the program coordinator explores financial support. These include student fees, fund-raising through development departments, and grants. Let's briefly explore these sources.

Additional Funding Resources

Student fees are a mechanism to raise additional revenue without increasing tuition. Depending on the governance of the institution, a student fee might be more prudent in a time when legislators and trustees are questioning tuition increases. Examples are technology fees, athletic fees, fine arts fees, laboratory fees, building fees, and student activity fees. There are two strategies for funding a program through student fees (Barr, 2002, 2016). First, review how the institution allocates student fees. There might be an opportunity to acquire support through funding for the project. For example, the student government at the institution might find the project to be a good investment for student activity fees. Thus, the program coordinator would follow the process to request financial support. Second, inquire whether or not the project meets campus guidelines for requesting a fee specific to the new program. Again, research the process, create the documents, and submit the material in a timely manner. On the campus of one author, new fee requests were reviewed by a committee twice a year. In addition to documents similar to the ones submitted for legislative funds, the program coordinator needed to make a formal presentation to the fee committee. Both options make student fees a source to consider when searching for resources.

Another avenue to fund a new program that is increasing in popularity across all areas of higher education is fund-raising, which is often done through the development office. By contacting department or division leaders, the program coordinator can become familiar with whether or not these private funds are available. If they are available, explore how to engage with the process of allocation. Often these funds emerge throughout the year, require understanding of the donors' interests, and lend themselves to programming that supports students. One element that is different with private funds is that the program coordinator might have the opportunity to talk directly to the donor about the program. This solicitation is often referred to as "the ask" and requires the right person to tell the narrative of the program. Once this solicitation occurs, the program coordinator needs to accept a period of silence as the donor processes the request. Because you are a caring campus partner, it is important to collaborate with the department, division, or campus development office if you pursue private funding. There are many guidelines, spoken and unspoken, about the solicitation process that the development office will be able to clarify (Barr, 2016; Wolf, 2016).

The final source to pursue for funding is a grant from a foundation. Foundations often advertise grants through development offices and an office of sponsored research. Each foundation is different in how it distributes funds based on a request. Some will have specific guidelines and foci for their financial resources whereas others are more open to a broader range of requests (Barr, 2002, 2016). It is important to read the announcement carefully and contact any resources that will increase understanding for a successful submission. Most grants for a foundation will have a preproposal deadline. After review of the preproposal by the foundation, requesting parties will be notified of further interest from the foundation and the process for submitting a grant proposal with a deadline. These grants are often one-time funds and accountability is important.

The budgeting process is another avenue for the program coordinator to fine-tune the program plan. It requires collaboration in identifying needs and resources for financial support. It includes writing a budget proposal as well as being able to articulate the opportunity for student success that these resources will bring to the campus. The last component of the budget is accountability, which the authors discuss in the following section.

Budget Accountability

Earlier in this chapter, we discussed the budget proposal and included a section on accountability. This section includes a brief review of the program assessment plan, budget oversight, procedures for monthly reconciliation, and sustainability measures to address accountability (Barr, 2002, 2016; Meisinger, 1994). Lasher and Greene (2001) stated that "a budget doubles as an accountability and control device, against which expenditures can be monitored for compliance" (p. 475). With this view of accountability being clearly stated, let's explore other techniques shared by the authors for communicating to stakeholders the impact these financial resources are having on the program as well as the greater community. Some people also refer to this as explaining the return on investment (ROI) made by the program.

Start with strategies and techniques that will not require expenditures other than time by the program coordinator or program staff. Social media tools are free and widely used in higher education. The key is consistency in posting, tweeting, or pinning, as well as interesting content. Social media is a quick way to share the impact the program has on one student or many. It also offers an opportunity to drive people to the program website for more details or stories that need additional space. Content on a blog or in a newsletter does double duty to different stakeholders based on which source they read.

Written content will be significant to certain audiences but photos and video also share a strong message. Does the campus have a media or communication department that needs content? Does the campus have a video project that is collecting information on campus programs that impact students and the community? Video is an opportunity to broaden campus partnerships while creating visual content for the website and social media outlets. It is important to consider the audiences who will appreciate this medium for addressing accountability on the budget allocation.

A picture may be worth a thousand words but never underestimate being on the program site or being involved in a program activity for your stakeholders. For example, if there is a program activity, such as a food collection party for the food pantry, invite stakeholders to join in the festivities. This offers an opportunity for stakeholders to understand the mission and goals of the program at the ground level. It also might be an opportunity to create content for other communication strategies.

As a program concludes each year, incorporate all accountability techniques into a comprehensive annual report. Through a combination of data and activities, the program coordinator writes the annual report to create the program narrative. Upon completion, the annual report is sent to key stakeholders, referred to when questions are asked about the program, and provides detailed and consistent data for future budget requests.

Even though the program coordinator and staff assume many tasks to produce a program, there are many reasons to encourage transparency in spending allocated resources that support accountability. As mentioned earlier in this chapter, the campus has limited revenue. There is constant competition for available revenue due to changes in the student population, fluctuating economic factors, and unexpected societal situations that result in new program proposals. Various forms of communication evidence that fiduciary responsibilities are taken seriously by the staff and leader of the program. Another reason to focus on accountability is potential budget cuts. A budget reduction might be campus-wide due to a reduction in a revenue stream or it might be focused on specific programs. Regardless of the reason for the reduction, managing the budget provides options during austere periods.

A number of the techniques for accountability increase communication about the program. Such communication creates an environment to enhance or develop new partnerships and allies. The team effect can result in not only maintaining current revenues but also identifying new revenue streams. Finally, accountability efforts set the stage for future budget cycles. Regardless of when the annual budget proposal is requested by the department, division, or university, the program coordinator has the materials to write the detail for a successful budget request (Barr, 2002, 2016; Meisinger, 1994).

Conclusion

This chapter has offered a broad overview of budgets and the budgeting process involved in stages of the IMPD. The definition of *budget* as well as the role of the budget in an organization provide a base understanding of the process of budgeting. The act of creating a budget proposal increases understanding of the proposed program in the program definition stage. It involves explaining program needs, researching prices for specific items, and collaborating with partners to outline all financial requirements to administer the program. The process for requesting funds varies based on which revenue stream (e.g., legislative funds, student fees, or private donors) the program coordinator pursues. Finally, it is paramount to embed accountability into the budget process as a tool to communicate fiscal responsibility, market the program, and prepare for future budget cycles. The budget impacts multiple stages of the IMPD, including the planning and monitoring stages. The next chapter offers other elements of the planning stage.

6

PROGRAM PLANNING AND MONITORING STAGES

Developing a Roadmap for the Program

After reading this chapter, you will be able to do the following:

1. Explain the planning and monitoring stages of the IMPD
2. Understand how theories and concepts inform the foundation of the program
3. Identify people engaged with the program as staff, stakeholders, planners, and participants
4. Create a timeline to follow from point of assignment to implementation
5. Develop a marketing plan to drive an audience to the program

The budget is a significant element in the IMPD, as communicated in the previous chapter. The fiscal component requires an unofficial cost-benefit analysis that verifies spending the resources on the program to meet the mission and goals of the unit or organization. Once a budget for a single idea or an entire unit is developed, submitted, reviewed, and accepted, it is time to outline how to move the idea to reality. The leader of the unit or organization will reinforce commitment to the proposed program by identifying a program coordinator. This individual assumes responsibility for the planning stage as well as other stages in the process. This chapter highlights key elements of the planning and monitoring stages of the IMPD, displayed in Figure 6.1.

This chapter begins with a reminder that scholarly literature and narratives of practice offer theories, frameworks, and ideas to create a foundation for the development of your plan. The literature might have been reviewed and synthesized within the budget proposal, but now that the program has

Figure 6.1. Integrated model for program development—Planning and monitoring.

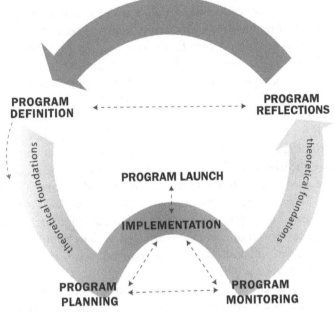

momentum, a comprehensive review of the literature will support the planning process. Then we address necessary components of the plan to deliver the program, which begins with identifying the scope of the project. The scope complements the goals and objectives (discussed in chapter 4) and increases understanding for stakeholders early in the planning stage, as you will read later in this chapter. Next, the chapter moves to the human element of the plan, comprising partners, stakeholders, and the team assigned to develop and deliver the program. A significant part of any plan is a timeline. Temporal and technology tools organize the tasks and people for a timely delivery of the program. Finally, a key element of the program plan for the activity, event, or service focuses on marketing to campus and community members. The activities focused on marketing motivate participation and action as this new opportunity emerges on the campus.

In addition to identifying key elements of a plan, the chapter will share examples that focus on planning a major fair, an annual campus event. Also, there are screenshots, such as a worksheet from a master spreadsheet that supports the planning and monitoring stages. The literature relevant to the topic of the program is a good place to start this chapter, as theoretical foundations offer a path for the model, as stated in chapter 1.

The Literature: Concepts and Theories

The field of higher education has a rich and deep body of literature that will inform you throughout the program planning process, but is especially significant as you develop the plan for the program. As the IMPD was introduced in chapter 1, it is clear that theories are foundational to the process. Thus, you might reach out to colleagues for recommendations or engage in a comprehensive review of the literature that starts with a campus librarian to identify key materials. This literature includes articles that create a history on the research for a topic or concept and explain theoretical frameworks that influence the topic. Also, the IMPD is built on a path that might involve one or more theories to build the program. Whether one theory or multiple theories are used, they provide structure, understanding, and a conceptual framework. An article by Bray and Major (2011), titled "Status of Journals in Higher Education," identifies a variety of journal titles that practitioners can reference to learn more about the topic or student population that the activity or program will address. It is important to spend time reading these articles to inform your project.

Books are another tool that communicates the scholarly literature. These nonfiction volumes explore a topic at a deeper level than an article and may incorporate more references than an article, due to the space available to describe and address the topic. In addition to a comprehensive literature review, a book might offer more detail on different viewpoints and describe programs to address the concept in greater detail. As you consider books to inform your planning, look for volumes that have been written by scholars and practitioners who study the topic and/or practice for the specific area. Also, use book reviews as a tool to evaluate the volume. A book review is often written by someone who is familiar with the broader literature around the topic, has read the book, and shares the strengths of the volume for future readers.

Even though journal articles and professional books are key for offering perspective and understanding, there are other tools to consider as you become the expert on the topic and plan a program for your campus. Many professional organizations offer practice-focused publications that specifically apply theory to practice through programming. A few examples are the ACPA publication called *Developments* and the NACADA publication called *Academic Advising Today* (NACADA, 2019). There are blogs that are written and posted by professional organizations, nonprofit organizations, academic departments, and individuals. A blog is a brief post that offers perspective on literature, research, and practice around the topic or focus of your program. Academic organizations, such as the Association for the Study of Higher Education (ASHE) and the American Educational Research Association (AERA), provide a venue for scholars and practitioners to present scholarly papers on research that often applies to practice. These scholarly papers are tools to inform you of the cutting edge research in the field. Finally, as you grow your network, you will meet scholars and practitioners who are delivering activities and programs that are of interest to you. Keep track of these individuals and their institutions through websites and social media feeds. This brief overview of written tools encourages you to read and reflect on the topic, concept, theory, and student population from the experiences of others. In addition to written tools, there are audio and video tools. A podcast is often a brief audio file delivered on a topic or concept produced by a wide variety of sources. Also, YouTube is one venue for video resources. All these tools will provide insight on what has worked and what has not produced anticipated results as you establish your program path with theoretical foundations. This wide variety of tools will inform your program plan, encourage innovation, and discourage reinventing a wheel that does not fit 21st-century higher education.

Here's a tip from those who have developed successful programs on how they use the literature: As you identify, read the literature, and listen to different perspectives, spend time considering the specific student populations that the program on your campus will impact. Every campus has a diverse student population based on a variety of salient identities held by the students. These identities include but are not limited to race/ethnicity, gender, sexual orientation, ability, age, socioeconomic status, first-generation, and commuter or rural geographic space. As you read about your topic or concept, track which student populations are being referenced in each piece of literature or media tool. Ask yourself if the program should consider different strategies based on the needs of various campus populations. Be careful to not generalize students as you plan for an activity or program that should impact student success.

As you are documenting concepts from the literature and their impact on students, you will also note other theories that emerge in this area of student engagement. Kerlinger (1986) described a *theory* as "a set of interrelated constructs, definitions, and propositions that presents a systematic view of phenomena by specifying relations among variables, with the purpose of explaining and predicting phenomena" (p. 9). Other synonyms for *theory* are *framework*, *proposition*, and *model*. Strayhorn (2016) clearly explained why theory is used by scholar-practitioners in our work of creating, developing, and delivering new programs. A theory supports the description of the program we are developing and assists in explaining certain elements of the program—for example, why the team decided to include a certain function or activity. Also, a theory offers opportunities to predict what might happen when infused with certain activities in a program or to produce a particular outcome that is tied to a goal. Assessment, covered in chapter 8, is an important element of any program and a theory can offer insight on how to frame the evaluation of learning that has emerged from the program. Finally, using a theory, framework, or model as we develop and plan a program offers a structure for future research to generate understanding and knowledge. If the program you are developing focuses on student development, you could start with a general text that offers a broad overview of many theories. As you read and theories emerge that offer an explanation for your program, explore each theory further. Using a theory, model, or conceptual framework as you develop a program is a good practice that connects your work to the larger field of student affairs. Thus, the IMPD clearly states that theoretical foundations offer a clear path for all stages of the model.

Also, the literature you read and notate will support you in developing a roadmap for the program and understanding theories and student populations; thus, it will influence the plan. You will be able to approach the idea from a place of knowledge and build a plan that supports you in delivering a program that meets your institutional mission and values. Figure 6.2 offers an example of literature that informs the topic of major exploration for the example of a major fair.

The following section revisits goals and objectives as the planning team contemplates the scope of the program in the planning stage.

Figure 6.2. Books and articles informing the planning stage of a major fair.

Glaessgen, T. A., MacGregor, C. J., Cornelius-White, J. H. D., Hornberger, R. S., & Baumann, D. M. (2018). First-generation students with undecided majors: A qualitative study of university reacculturation. *NACADA Journal, 38*(1), 22–35.

Gordon, V. N. (2007). *The undecided student: An academic and career advising challenge* (3rd ed.). Charles C. Thomas.

Gordon, V. N., & Sears, S. J. (2009). *Selecting a college major: Exploration and decision making* (6th ed.). Pearson.

Soria, C. M., & Stebleton, M. (2013). Major decisions: Motivations for selecting a major, satisfaction, and belonging. *NACADA Journal, 33*(2), 29–43.

Scope: A Complement to Goal and Objective

A key element of program development is identifying the goal that the program will accomplish. Chapter 4 offered understanding for developing goals, objectives, and learning outcomes, which are often initiated as the program is being defined. This earlier chapter offered depth and breadth on all three concepts. As you, the program coordinator, and the program team move into the planning and monitoring stages, you might want to review and continuously focus on these components. This behavior will guarantee that the program is addressing the desired purpose.

It is also recommended to identify clearly the scope of the activity or program. Oxford Dictionary defines *scope* as "the extent of the area or subject matter that something deals with or to which it is relevant" (Lexico, n.d.). By applying this definition to the IMPD early in the planning stage, scope will provide clarity for the goal and identify the parameters of the program under development. Let's look at an example of a program goal for Welcome Week from chapter 4. One program goal articulated in the chapter was "to encourage students new to campus to join campus clubs and organizations" (p. 54, this volume). Once you have this goal, a scope can follow that offers direction and boundaries. In this example, the focus is on campus clubs for students with the aim of encouraging new students to become involved. Thus, recruitment for faculty or staff clubs or off-campus organizations is not the focus or part of the parameters for the event.

We offer another example of goal and scope via the campus food pantry example. If the main goal is "enhancing student wellness," the scope might read as "enhancing student wellness through establishing a campus food pantry." The scope provides a level of detail that offers clear direction in delivery of a food pantry and establishes the parameters that it is for student wellness, with a location on the campus for easy student access.

Why is a scope significant to the planning process? First, the level of detail shared through the scope offers direction for the planning stage, including the timeline. In the second example shown, it is clear that wellness will be addressed through a campus food pantry. Second, the scope establishes parameters for accomplishing the goal by supplying food through a food pantry on the campus. Returning to the example, wellness is specifically approached through a service on the campus and not in the larger community. In this case, the scope is significant in identifying what will happen and where it will happen. As the program emerges through the planning stage, the scope offers direction as well as justification for certain actions. By stating these details early in the process, progress is made toward accomplishing the goal through development and delivery of the program without delay caused by ambiguity.

Ambiguity in program definition and planning slows down progress and offers opportunities for various stakeholders to redirect the program. This redirection might include expanding the program as far as services or audience. The use of the IMPD encourages the establishment of key details, such as goals, budget, and scope, early in the program definition and planning stages to avoid this redirection and to prevent failing to accomplish the organizational mission. For example, in the previous example—"enhancing student wellness through establishing a campus food pantry"—a lack of scope might redirect resources for a campus food pantry to recreation facilities or student counseling. The scope offers clear direction for how resources will be used to accomplish wellness.

One of the authors learned early in her career that a clear statement of scope is critical. She recalls one example of a new service area being developed with the following scope: Enhance student retention through frontline practitioners roving the campus to directly talk to students in their environments. As the planning evolved, she was confronted with offers of office space to house these individuals in exchange for the personnel accomplishing administrative duties in the area. The scope of being mobile to talk with students in their campus space justified declining these offers of space and kept the focus on direct student contact in spaces traversed by students.

An additional note regarding scope focuses on responding to institutional change. A clear scope offers agility to respond to the unexpected and a starting point for innovation. As we write this book, the world is experiencing a pandemic. In-person higher education institutions moved quickly to online environments, and programs that included various degrees of human contact were forced to rethink how to function in the online environment or decide to postpone to a later date or completely cancel. A clear scope provided direction to rework the program definition and planning stage for possible delivery. These reconfigured programs honored policies, rules, and guidelines issued by various levels of government to address health and human safety. Some programs changed procedures while others changed modality for interaction. Let's look at a few examples, starting with a campus food pantry. Some institutions determined that those students who needed access to the pantry would submit food request orders via a technology tool. Campus food pantry staff and volunteers, outfitted in masks, rubber gloves, and other appropriate protective clothing, collected and bagged food for orders. Then the bags were delivered to safe and agreed-on points for students to collect, again following all protocol for safety and social distancing.

Another example is from one of the authors. A program on his campus offers the opportunity for prospective graduate students to meet department chairs in an on-campus format to learn about the vast range of academic opportunities. This in-person event in the Los Angeles, California, area could not occur due to COVID-19 restrictions. The scope of the program was clear, and through the use of ZOOM (a video conferencing platform) the chairs met with the students. Additionally, due to a feature in ZOOM that allows the large group to break into smaller groups, all students had virtual engagement with each chair for detailed conversations and to address specific questions. Both examples convey the message that if program definition and scope are clear, the program coordinator and team will be able to adjust to deliver the program. Finally, in the process of program development, the goal and scope are tools that offer clear direction for the timeline, too. Another tool that informs the plan is the stakeholder who serves as staff, collaborators, partners, participants, donors, and planning team members.

Collaboration and Partnership

The development of a new program, whether an event that happens once a year or a group of events or services that happen continuously throughout a year, needs different forms of resources. A key resource for the sponsor of a program and the program coordinator is colleagues who support you in thinking through the details and logistics. These colleagues might be experts on the topic on another campus, partners in your campus division or unit, faculty interested in the topic, or students who have requested the program. Regardless of their assigned location, they will be critical to itemizing needs and developing a timeline in the planning stage. The chapter on budget provides further information on how to use this unofficial working group to identify basic logistical needs and then translate those needs into a budget request.

There are four other reasons to include a group of people in the program development process besides drawing on their expertise to develop a budget and support program success. First, this group of people will be able to identify other campus events. Especially in a time of limited resources, it is important to not create new programs that mimic or duplicate existing programs, and it is essential that a new program does not compete with an existing program, especially a popular one. Second, these colleagues offer more than their subject and campus expertise; they might offer a resource or identify a way to collaborate that enriches the new program. Third, by including others in the planning process, we are building buy-in and beginning the marketing of the program. Fourth, most programs need a team of people to plan, monitor, and implement. This team might be a collection of people within your organization as well as campus partners. Once the team is formed, the program will gain a new level of momentum when it becomes clear that collaboration has many benefits for planning the program. People, whether seasoned practitioners and faculty or new comers to the institution, are critical to the program development process. This point is stressed throughout the book as people interact to engage in the stages of IMPD. Another critical element of planning that relates to human resources is staff.

Hiring, Training, and Supervising Staff

A quick review of the budget will indicate if the program has been allocated financial resources for permanent staff to deliver the program. These types of resources are allocated for programs that will function every day to deliver a service. Many books have been written on hiring, training, and supervising staff that should be referenced before hiring. Also, the program coordinator should interact with all campus resources that support human resources. This chapter will offer a few key points to support the IMPD.

Not all new programs require hiring new staff. The needs analysis offered in chapter 3 is important for making this decision. Also the introduction in chapter 5 offers a scenario on new programs that did not require new staff since the programs were annual and fit into the work routine of the sponsoring unit. It is important to evaluate the need early since this element is a significant budget request.

As you identify funding for a staff member (if the program requires staff), review the original program proposal. What will this staff member be responsible for in the future? As you answer this question, you will create a key document filled with responsibilities that identify the position classification and job title. A conversation with human resources or the human capital office will support you in identifying whether this position type and classification already exists at your institution or if a new position must be created. In either case the position description communicates what is expected as well as the skills and abilities needed for the position. Once the description is clear, you can post the position for hiring.

Every campus has a process for hiring new staff. Continue to work with human resources as well as your program team to identify and follow the process. Look for opportunities to advertise the position to produce a quality pool of applicants that not only have the appropriate skill set but also are diverse. It is important to spend time reviewing the applications with a search committee that is vested in hiring a new colleagues committed to the institutional mission.

Upon hiring the new staff, have a well-developed process for onboarding the new campus members. This includes meeting people, completing all campus hiring documents, and participating in training that will offer context for the position and campus. It is important to convene regular meetings with the new staff members to follow up on their training and needs. The authors encourage you to engage early and often with new staff members to create a sense of belonging for short- and long-term retention. Include the staff members in the program planning activities and the team as soon as possible. The program coordinator should assign program tasks to the new staff members that will complement training activities, offer engagement with the implementation team, and allow them to demonstrate their competency. The process of hiring staff is an important element that should be addressed as early as possible in the planning stage of the program. It is a key part of planning the work that will produce a timeline. Also, once staff are hired, the training and development of staff are part of the monitoring stage. The program coordinator should be clear on assignments for the developing program, engage in regularly scheduled meetings with the staff on assignments, and follow up on all questions. Through these interactions, the program coordinator will provide necessary training that supports staff in growing skills and confidence to implement the program plan and meet deadlines in the timeline.

Planning the Work—The Timeline

The IMPD outlines stages in a detailed process that requires the program sponsor and/or program coordinator to think deeply about all aspects of the program. You might compare program development to planning a trip in your car. There are specific tasks for a trip, such as acquiring directions and purchasing fuel, that need to occur at specific times to accomplish the goal. Program development also requires attention to task and time as you initiate the program. At this point, in addition to a budget, you have identified the following pieces of information for your program:

- The goal and scope of the program, which include the student population(s) the program is intended to impact through in-person, online, or a hybrid environment
- The theory that is guiding your work from the literature you read and people you spoke with as you were exploring this new program
- Personnel involved in development, implementation, and ongoing delivery

- Logistical details such as venue, equipment, and technology
- Operational items for specific activities such as food, swag, transportation or travel, office supplies, and/or honorariums

Now let's think about the time allotted and establish a timeline that incorporates all the details necessary to deliver the program.

It is highly recommended that the program coordinator develop a timeline and then embed that timeline into spreadsheet software. The spreadsheet, as well as all program documents, should be saved in a file that lives on a shared drive or cloud storage for easy access. The timeline will serve as a guide to make sure actions happen in a timely manner. Some leaders will also create a calendar visible in a well-traveled space for all members of the team to view on a regular basis as well as build into the calendar key activities including celebration activities that occur as certain milestones are accomplished by the team. Spreadsheet software offers an opportunity to identify specific needs, attach a completion date, make assignments to a staff or faculty member, note when the task is completed, and indicate any special issues or concerns for future iterations of the program (see Figure 6.3). Also, there is specific software for program development (e.g., Trello), which you might opt to use depending on the size of the program. We advise that you take time to investigate these products to find a good match between your needs and the software features. Also, consider campus tools that are easily accessible. These electronic tools are key to effective program development and support the stages of planning, monitoring, and implementing in the IMPD.

The timeline organizes the logistical and operational details. Before you begin to build the timeline for your program, ask stakeholders to brainstorm key activities that occur annually on your campus that might have an impact on the timeline for the new program. This list might include annual fairs (e.g., study abroad, wellness, or career fairs), student activities (e.g., homecoming events, winter socials, or conferences), or other major campus events (e.g., commencement, college/department retreats, final exams). Also consider the overall academic calendar that will identify when classes begin and end, breaks during the term, deadlines for key policy issues (e.g., last day to withdraw), and final exam schedules. Finally, if your campus has a campuswide calendar, review it for potential activities that might conflict with your activities or as a tool to identify periods that have fewer activities to compete with your program. Now that you have a clear understanding of the campus landscape for events, identify the completion or delivery date of your program. Once this date is established, the program planning team members brainstorm activities for implementing the program and establish completion dates that are spread over months, weeks, and days. By incorporating the institutional knowledge of colleagues, students, and other partners as well as looking at established calendars, you will craft a timeline that offers the least amount of conflict and the greatest opportunity for success.

Next you need to evaluate the type of program and how you apply a program development timeline to it. Is this a one-time event that requires certain actions to happen at certain times and culminates in the activity occurring once or twice a year for a short period of time? This program is developing an annual event with specific goals. Some examples are career fairs, scholarship dinners, and leadership conferences. The other common type of program is a new service that will be available on a regular basis throughout the year. For the purpose of discussing the timeline, this program type will be referred to as continuous service event. Continuous service events might be a food pantry, wellness center, or childcare center. After you understand the campus calendar, established events, and the type of program you are developing, you begin to draft your timeline. It is important to remember that your initial assessment of needs, covered in chapter 3, will indicate how often this program is offered on the campus.

This time-oriented tool will identify key dates attached to tasks that need to be completed and the required personnel to accomplish the event. As mentioned previously, the timeline is best communicated through spreadsheet software that offers columns and rows for clear communication of not only dates and tasks but also who is assigned to a task, costs, and notes for future iterations of the program. It is paramount that the team of people invited to develop and implement this program have access to the spreadsheet with the timeline continuously. Thus, it should be posted in an accessible location. Many teams use virtual storage spaces, such as Google Drive, Dropbox, or Box. These virtual spaces offer everyone access for a quick reference, and an opportunity to contribute to the timeline and spreadsheet with relevant information. This tool, such as a spreadsheet, is in a virtual space that encourages transparency in the program development process. The program coordinator must delegate activities and the spreadsheet is a great tool for recording these assignments. Due to the timeline and other details, the spreadsheet communicates the responsibilities for each team member as well as the date they must be accomplished to guarantee an on-time delivery. Because the program spreadsheet identifies who has been assigned a task, the program coordinator or designee will routinely review the spreadsheet to guarantee completion of assignments. These actions orchestrate team and individual accountability, which is necessary for timely program delivery. Let's apply these tools to an example of an annual event—a major fair.

Timeline of Annual Event—Major Fair

A major fair is an annual or semiannual activity that allows students to explore all academic program options in one convenient space for a short period of time. It is usually assigned to an established unit or division so as not to require additional personnel. The budget is submitted to support the activity through the unit or division process. The program coordinator and, possibly, the program team need to begin with some basic questions that inform stages in the IMPD. Table 6.1 identifies the questions and relationship to stages.

This approach uses time periods focused around the event for organization and structure. This structure is also a great way to organize the spreadsheet for the event. Let's begin with a simple question: What needs to happen to plan this event? As the planning stage begins, the committee needs to focus on basic requirements and necessities to bring this program to delivery. The committee will identify these requirements with the following themes and questions that focus on the major fair program:

- Location
  - Where will the program occur? Is the venue online, in-person or mixed? Does the space require a reservation? When is it available? Will it accommodate the activity and number of people participating?
- People and participants
  - Who will participate in the program?
  - Do we need to have anyone RSVP or reserve a space?
- Equipment
  - Do we need special equipment? Is it available at the current venue?

TABLE 6.1
Program Development Questions and IMPD Stages to Craft a Timeline

Question	IMPD Stage
What needs to happen to plan this event?	Planning, monitoring, and implementing
What needs to happen during the event to accomplish the program goals?	Implementing and launching
What needs to happen after the event as planning for the next iteration of the program?	Reflecting

- Food
  - Do we need to offer food and/or drink? If so, how will we identify a vendor?
  - Have we accommodated for a variety of dietary needs for the guests?
  - Are we using sustainable practices that address environmental issues?
- ADA compliance
  - Are the space reserved for the event, advertising materials, and materials for the event (e.g., program) ADA-compliant?

The major fair program offers an example to address these questions.

If you are offering this event in a real-time format, the major fair needs a space or location. Next, estimate the number of academic programs that may request a table. By calculating the size of the space, you will be able to identify sites that will accommodate the activity. Once potential sites have been identified, look at cost and availability. Most campuses have some type of large ballroom or multipurpose room. These spaces offer a variety of amenities such as tables, chairs, decorations, and sound systems. A team member should research these elements of the location as well as cost and availability and report to the team or program coordinator. When the team identifies and reserves the space for a specific date, the delivery target is clear and planning for other elements of the program can begin. Next, the team will review questions to establish other tasks that must be accomplished. Figure 6.3 identifies some of these tasks, with a date for completion, that emerge in the "Major Fair—October 15 (Planning & Monitoring)" worksheet.

Now that the timeline for the major fair program is initiated to guarantee an on-time delivery, let's turn our attention to another significant element of the planning stage—marketing to engage participants for the program.

Marketing—Motivating People to Participate

Someone needs to take responsibility for marketing the program. This should be a team discussion. Due to the importance of program success through participation, the program coordinator might assume this responsibility, or a small subteam or another team member who has special knowledge or networks for marketing. Be specific on who will lead the marketing effort. The planning team needs to identify the campus and community participants for the program. Once these key populations are identified, the team needs to initiate communication that motivates participation. Marketing becomes

Figure 6.3. Timeline emerges in planning and monitoring event worksheet for major fair.

	A	B	C	D	E	F
1	**Major Fair—October 15 (Planning & Monitoring)**					
2	Team: Dayan (Chair), Luis, David, Kim, and Michelle					
3	**Activity**	**Deadline**	**Assigned to**	**Cost**	**Note**	**Complete**
4	Identify Venue	Jan. 1	Kim	$200 includes tables & 2 chairs Note: 80 tables available	Book room at least one year in advance for specific date	Yes
5	Dayan visits Cliff Univ. to observe a major fair	Dec. 1	Dayan	$ 400.00	Airfare and hotel for one night	Yes
6	Team spends time at campus career fair	Feb. 28	Team	$ 100.00	Team lunch to discuss what we viewed	Yes
7	Invite academic departments	Mar. 15	Luis			Yes
8	Attend advisor committee	Mar. 1	Luis			Yes
9	Send email to advisor listserv	Mar. 3	Luis			Yes
10	Develop RSVP form as fillable PDF	Feb. 28	Luis			Yes
11	Develop layout for fair	Sept. 1	Kim			
12	Market to students—orientation	May 30–July 15	David	Flyers & swag for tabling - $300	*Parents showed more interest *Better swag	Yes
13	Market to students—beginning of school events	Aug. 25–31	David	Flyers & swag for tabling - $300		
14	Market to students—campus paper	Sept. 15–Oct. 15	David	$10/daily ad	Expensive—Ask on evaluation how students learned of event	
15	Market to students—social media	Continuous	Michelle			

◄ ► ►	**Planning & Monitoring**	Implementing	Launching	Reflecting	⊕

another element of the plan that advertises the program to campus communities to encourage participation.

The American Marketing Association (2013) stated, "Marketing is the activity, set of institutions, and processes for creating, communicating, delivering, and exchanging offerings that have value for customers, clients, partners, and society at large" (para. 2). There are volumes written on this activity. Besides creating awareness of the program through marketing, what else is possible? Let's explore the power of stories in all aspects of your marketing as well as look at campus resources to support marketing.

Push-Pull Marketing

Gallagher and Thordarson (2018) shared a marketing strategy called "push-pull" that is used by many companies such as Apple. They used an analogy of a carrot and stick, with pushing being the stick and pulling being the carrot. The act of pushing is identifying a commodity or event to someone and insisting they should buy it now. Pulling is creating a need and building relationships that allow people to find the product or event. The act of pulling motivates people to actively engage because they clearly see a need is being met through the program. The key to this motivation is a well-communicated story by a trusted source that offers choices.

Education is filled with stories if we take the time to dialogue, listen, and share. This facilitation of an organic exchange among stakeholders and constituents creates a synergy for innovation. The dialogue identifies not only challenges but also opportunities for change. From the dialogue, stories will emerge that pull campus community members into participating, not because they have to but because they see value in meeting personal needs, want to positively impact student success, and want to support the institutional mission.

In addition to human stories with rich meaning that connect to the program, data are also compelling pieces of evidence to secure support and draw people to participate in the program. It is important to carefully consider how you communicate your message with both mediums. The team involved in delivering the program should ask the following questions during the program planning stage to address marketing:

- Who are the participants for this program? Do they have the same role in participating or are they different? Is there more than one population or campus constituency?
- How does each group take in information?
- How do we identify stories and data to use for marketing that will create understanding and trust?
- Who is responsible for marketing the program?
- What campus resources will support marketing by "pulling" these populations into program participation?

These questions will drive the team to craft a marketing plan for a successful event. Marketing should use a theme to create a common point of identification or brand for the event or service, in addition to strategic stories and data.

Before returning to the example of the major fair, let's identify marketing resources that are available on many campuses. A communication or media office is a great resource to support you in building the plan with stories, data, and a common theme. Once this is done, the program planning team and those responsible for marketing need to identify locations to communicate the event with the marketing tools developed, such as with the following options:

- Communication or media office for the university or college with access to a local or national news feed
- Campus newspaper or radio station
- Daily or weekly bulletins or announcements
- Electronic mailing list for specific groups
- Social media that is facilitated by the university, college, division, and/ or department
- Websites with images and video
- Banners displayed in key areas
- Flyers, email messages, and text messages

Going back to the literature and the institutional mission, try to understand the audience and what motivates them to engage. Many campus events or services are designed for students as the target audience. Thus, it is important to understand which specific population of students your program is designed for and then identify the location and tool to share effective stories that attract the population by communicating a need that will be met.

Marketing for the Major Fair

Now it is time to apply marketing to the major fair example. During the planning and implementation stages, the planning team identifies two groups of stakeholders for participation. These groups are the students exploring majors, minors, and certificates for their degree program and representatives, such as academic advisers, from academic departments. To begin, it is important to consider what might appeal as a common visual across the marketing to tie the advertising pieces together and create focused and repeated communication about the event. After discussion with committed partners and campus experts, it is decided to use bright-colored puzzle pieces with a bright yellow background across all communication as a branding strategy. Next, consolidate the stories, data, and brand into materials that are shared with academic departments and students. Let's start with the academic department. The marketing message to the department communicates how this fair will meet a student need, which is finding a major. Strong stories of students leaving the college or university due to not finding their major or the success of a fair on another campus can facilitate the "pull" strategy with quality stories. Also, share data that motivate departments to participate, such as the number of undeclared students who are enrolled on the campus. In addition to the story told through experiences and real data, it is imperative that detailed communication be sent to departments to clarify how to participate and a request for an RSVP.

Next, it is vital to know how your campus communicates this type of information. Is it best to send an email to a specific person? Are there campus organizations, such as a campus-wide advising organization, that you could address and distribute information? Once you identify communication outlets, use them continuously. Through a campus committee, listserv, email, flyers, and social media feed, the major fair planning committee attracted 93% of the academic departments to the first event. As departments informed the team of their intentions to participate, the layout of the space started to take shape for the actual day of the event.

Naturally, the other campus stakeholders who are important to this process are students, especially students who are exploring majors. Through the literature on major exploration and students who are exploring majors, the planning team and campus marketing resources developed the marketing plan for students. The same image of puzzle pieces for the brand was used across a number of communication tools and spaces. These activities included tabling at events such as orientation and Welcome Week, emails to students who had not declared a major, social media posts about the event, visits to first-year classes, and large banners displayed throughout the campus. The committee also asked faculty to share the event with students because the literature clearly indicates that students involve themselves in programs and events that are advertised by faculty. Once the marketing plan was activated, departments were reserving tables and students were adding this to their activities for October. The planning committee for the major fair began to consider other details about the location and activities as the planning moved closer to the day of the event.

Concluding the Roadmap

This chapter covered key elements to consider as you create the plan that moves the program coordinator and team through the planning and monitoring stages to the implementing and launching stages for the program. Elements in these stages are engaging with the literature; identifying the scope to complement the goal; collaborating with a variety of people in the community; and building a specific team of people to develop and deliver a structured plan with a timeline that is incorporated into a spreadsheet with assignments for accountability and marketing. Now it is time to think about the "little extras" that will move the event from average to phenomenal. These items might include elements of fun, such as prizes for best booth, or providing for a student need such as food. Make the event inviting with music and colorful with balloons or other fun materials. What will draw people in who have not seen your marketing? Maybe the popcorn machine or the campus mascot, which appeal to people's senses. A good plan addresses the basic needs and then elevates to go beyond expectations. The monitoring stage includes tracking of these details on the spreadsheet and is important to this model.

As people work the plan, the date for delivery is flashing on the calendar as well as through social media venues for both the planning team and campus community. Just like a good roadmap indicates turns, mileage, and route numbers for a successful trip, following the IMPD indicates when it is time to move from planning and monitoring stages to the implementation stage. In the next chapter, we'll move to the implementation and launch stages and continue on the program development journey with details outlined initially in the implementation worksheet.

IMPLEMENTATION AND LAUNCH STAGES

Lights, Camera, Action

After reading this chapter, you will be able to do the following:

1. Describe key elements of the implementation and launch stages of the IMPD
2. Develop a work flow that is focused on details for implementation and program delivery
3. Identify and develop training activities that support the program and the staff
4. Identify strategies to celebrate the team's accomplishment

This chapter will focus on key elements of the implementation stage as well as the program launch stage in the IMPD. Let's begin with a scenario to understand the details and deadlines that emerge in these stages.

It is one week before the program launches. I am looking at the "to do" list from the program worksheet and the budget. I keeping asking myself, "Has the program team thought of everything?" As I glance again at the budget with 437 line items, Jeff walks in and asks if we have a broom in the budget. It takes me a minute to comprehend the question. Jeff repeats himself. "Do we need to buy a broom?" As I emerge from my daze, I respond, "We didn't, but if you think we need one, we can add it." Quickly Jeff grabs a donut, looks at the master calendar of program activities, and shares, "I just visited the venue and they provide no tools or materials for routine clean-up. A broom will be pretty handy as well as some window cleaner and paper towels." I endorse the suggestion, make a note for a purchase from the operation budget, and add to the "Implementing Event" worksheet a note to buy cleaning supplies. The entire team is engaged with their assignments, which is guaranteeing a smooth delivery as well as addressing details that we missed in early stages of planning the event.

As the vignette describes, the date of delivery approaches quickly as the program plan goes into motion. You and the team finalize all essential details, such as space, equipment, and human participation, and continue to build a strategic list of activities to deliver the event or service. Now it is time to organize the implementation, which is a significant stage in the IMPD (see Figure 7.1).

Back to our spreadsheet and look for worksheets labeled "Implementing Event" and "Launching Event." These worksheets assign tasks to your team that happen immediately before or during the launch of the program. The timespan is down to weeks, days, and hours, but your team is ready. Why? First, you have a detailed plan with a work flow that addresses all areas of the program. Second, you have invested time identifying the training the staff needs to deliver the program. Third, you have identified opportunities to celebrate the team's accomplishment. These are all key elements of a program as it moves from planning to production.

Figure 7.1. Integrated model for program development—Implementation and launch.

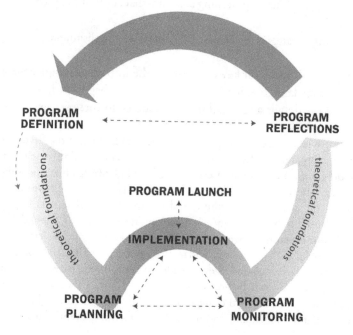

Organizing for Implementation and Launch of the Program

Organizational skill will be increasingly important as the date of implementation grows closer. There are many moving pieces that need attention by the program coordinator and the program team. Tools that were implemented earlier, such as a budget, spreadsheets, and calendar, are updated to address program logistics within appropriate time periods. We suggest creating two more worksheets in the master spreadsheet. The first worksheet focuses on implementation and will cover 4 to 6 weeks before the event or program launch. The second worksheet will address activities for the day of launch.

The program coordinator and team will continuously review all worksheets at each meeting. Each meeting will focus on program logistics and will be recorded through a tape recorder and/or written minutes. Regardless of the method, it is important to transfer specific activities to the worksheets. Make sure the tasks are recorded accurately, with names of team members to whom tasks are assigned, dates by which tasks must be accomplished, and any specific details such as vendor for pickup or contact name. Especially with a new program, all worksheets will continue to grow at each meeting as certain tasks require a subtask or new information that impacts the program is discovered by a team member.

The "Implementing Event" worksheet focuses on activities that happen weeks before the event. The program coordinator begins this worksheet by reviewing items on the "Planning Event" worksheet. As the event draws closer, the level of detail is enhanced with specific tasks that impact delivery of the program on the anticipated date:

- Confirming with vendors specific details on delivery date
- Walking through the venue used for the program or event
- Testing software programs critical for delivery
- Creating a layout of the venue for participants
- Finalizing decorations
- Reminding participants of the event
- Sending informational materials (e.g., videos) to participants for maximum satisfaction
- Finalizing catering details, including ordering food
- Finalizing assessment tools
- Training personnel who are responsible for delivering the program

An organized planning team will deliver on time and be able to navigate last-minute challenges. Figure 7.2 identifies activities that are included in the implementation event worksheet for the major fair.

Figure 7.2. Activities included on implementing event worksheet for major fair.

	A	B	C	D	E	F	G
1	**Major Fair—October 15 (Implementing)**						
2	Team: Dayan (Chair), Luis, David, Kim, and Michelle						
3	Activity	Deadline	Assigned to	Cost	Note	Complete	
4	Decorations **order balloons	Sept. 1	Luis	$ 100.00		Yes	
5	Walk through venue and discuss layout	Sept. 15	Team	$ 100.00	Lunch for team at meeting to discuss tasks and assignments	Yes	
6	Training developed by Dayan for all teams	Oct. 1	Dayan & David	$ 100.00	Breakfast & training for 2 hrs.		
7	Market to students—social media	Continuous	Michelle		Run a new post twice a day on each platform		
8	Market to students—campus paper	Oct. 1	David	$ 150.00	Expensive—Ask on evaluation how students learned of event		
9	Layout for the room	Oct. 1	Kim		Make sure this goes to Alisa		
10	Send reminder to representative from academic dept.	Oct. 7	Luis		Include logistics of setup, lunch, takedown		
11	Create video on tabling for maximum benefit	Sept. 15	Michelle			Yes	
12	Post video on tabling to website and on social media	Sept. 16	Michelle				
13	Send update with video on effective tabling	Sept. 16	Luis				
14	Order lunch for representatives	Sept. 16	Luis	$ 666.00	Box lunch = $9 74 representatives Total=$666		
15	Order lunch pizza & cookies for students	Sept. 16	Luis	$ 450.00	Anticipating 1000 students/order 50 pizza/$8@ and 25 dozen cookies/$2@doze n Total=$450		
16	Reserve popcorn machine and supplies	Sept. 15	David	$ 100.00	Makes enough popcorn for 500 bags	Yes	
	Planning & Monitoring		Implementing		Launching	Reflecting	

In addition to developing a worksheet that supports program details weeks before the program begins, it is important to organize activities for the day of the launch. As explained previously, the team will discuss what needs to happen on the day of the event and refer back to worksheets focused on the planning and implementation stages. Relevant tasks should be recorded in a worksheet that is labeled "Launching Event."

The launch event worksheet is detailed and direct. Some major differences between this worksheet and the previous worksheets are notation of time and the increase of team members to deliver the program. Previous worksheets for planning and implementation arranged the temporal element by dates first and a time if necessary. On launch day, it is important to choreograph the tasks by specific hours and minutes. Why? First, you need to make sure events and activities occur as communicated to the participants and clients. Thus, you need to think about not only when it will occur but also how long it will take. Also, build in a time buffer to accommodate unexpected situations. Doors not unlocked, tables not in place, slow catering, or snow in September are just a few of the many situations we have experienced on delivery day of programs. The program coordinator and team who start a task early and allocate a small amount of extra time for each task will not be overwhelmed by any unexpected situations. They will have time to work through it to deliver on time.

The second reason for a finer grain of detail is to identify the number of people you will need to deliver the program. In the example of the major fair, the team of five could not accomplish all program launch tasks in a timely manner. Thus, they learned that the team needed to grow and then delegate specific activities to new members of the team. How does the team grow? The opportunity to invite people to participate on the launch day is a great strategy for promoting the activity, increasing the collective skill set of the group, and identifying new ideas for future iterations of the program. Figure 7.3 offers an example of activities for the launching stage of a major fair.

All the worksheets on the master spreadsheet communicate the vast number of tasks that must be completed before the event occurs or services open for an on-time delivery. Thus, it is imperative that the program coordinator and planning team delegate tasks to each other and any subteams (e.g., the launch day team) and that people accept responsibility for each assignment. Routine meetings are a time to monitor assignments. This form of continuous check-in with staff allows for celebration of completed assignments as well as conversations on challenges that are impeding progress. The program coordinator should encourage the team to discuss and develop solutions. Keep dialogue flowing as the program comes to life. As you add people, it is important to offer training and clear expectations of their roles. The training and development of people on the program team will be covered in the next section of the chapter.

Figure 7.3. Activities included on launching event worksheet for a major fair.

	A	B	C	D	E	F	G
1	**Major Fair—October 15 (Launching)**						
2	**Team: Dayan (Chair), Luis, David, Kim, and Michelle.**						
3	**Launch Day Team: Luis (leader), Zitlalli, Gerardo, Amy, Jason, Chris, Paul, Pat, Rich, and Deb**						
4	**Activity**	**Oct. 15**	**Assigned to**	**Cost**	**Notes**	**Complete**	
5	Pick up balloons	8:00 AM	Dayan				
6	Balloons distributed in venue	8:45 AM	Dayan and Kim				
7	Set up venue *Signs on table, welcome bag, sign holder	8:00 AM	Luis will lead team of 10		Dept. representatives arrive at 9 AM		
8	Layout followed for dept. signs on tables	8:00 AM	Jill				
9	Make popcorn for students	9:00 AM	Michelle				
10	Clean up popcorn machine	2:00 PM	Michelle				
11	Handout popcorn to students	All day	Michelle will create a sign-up		Rotate 2 people every hr.		
12	Surveys	All day	Dayan		Rotate Launch Team every hr.		
13	Food delivery as planned	9 AM Coffee & Donuts	David				
14	Food delivery as planned	11:30 Lunch	David				
15	Music in venue sound system	9:00 AM	Kim				
16	Welcome dept. representatives and direct to table	9:00 AM	Luis will lead team of 10				
17	Disassemble venue	2:15 PM	Luis will lead team of 10				

Planning & Monitoring | Implementing | Launching | Reflecting ⊕

Training and Developing Staff in Planning, Implementing, and Launching a Program

As the vignette at the beginning of the chapter communicates, it is the human factor that not only generates an idea but also brings the idea to life through the IMPD. In the scenario, as Jeff accomplishes one assignment, he identifies some tools that need to be purchased and shares this with a team member. The creation of the program through the tasks listed in the planning and monitoring worksheet is continued evidence that people are important to this process. Some programs will use current staff for planning, implementation, and launch whereas other programs will require the hiring of staff. The process of assigning people to support program delivery as well as hiring was covered in chapter 6. The implementation and launch stages of the IMPD require the program coordinator to focus on training and development for the specific assignments.

Training—What Do You Need

One responsibility of the program coordinator is to identify the training needed by team members to deliver the program. The amount and type will depend on the type of program. A one-day event such as a major fair is quite different from initiating a service such as a student success center. Thus, it is important to think about training to accomplish physical tasks and to develop content knowledge necessary to accomplish the program goal and contribute to the institutional mission.

The implementation and delivery of most programs require specific physical tasks. An important responsibility of the program coordinator is to identify the tasks and provide appropriate training to ensure task completion. Let's review some strategies to identify tasks that also inform training requirements: existing programs at other institutions, similar programs at your institution, and literature in the field that describes the program.

Many times, a professional development opportunity, such as a conference, has brought a program to your attention. Thus, some form of the program exists at another institution. If so, the program coordinator should initiate communication that offers access to planning documents that include training tools. Also there might be opportunity to include the team in reviewing these documents and having a virtual conversation with other institutions currently offering the program. Some people indicate that observing the event or service and talking to staff and students is a great opportunity to see the vision as well as identify specific details relevant to their campus and mission. In this case a visit to the campus can be effective for planning as well as real-time training. If the campus is close enough to your campus, you might turn this into a field trip for the program planning team. All of these strategies offer different types of opportunities to create your list of tasks for the planning, implementation, and launch worksheets based on viewing the actual event or service.

We congratulate you if the program is unique enough that you would not find models on other campuses. We also suggest that you look closer to home to see if your institution offers an event or service with some similarities that might serve as an adequate model for planning and training. For example, any type of real-time, annual event to share information with undergraduate students for increased institutional retention might benefit from observing a major or career fair as well as talking to those who plan and deliver the event. The topic might be different but often the venue, vendors, participants, and training are the same. Thus, the overlap of tasks and assignments around marketing, setting up the venue, and assessing the program would initiate the planning process.

Finally, the literature in the field is another source for descriptions of programs that would impact a task list as well as offering staff development. These are often short articles written by practitioners in the field who have accomplished the task. The level of description is often dependent on the submission guidelines. If the level of detail you need is not present, the name of the author is available for future contact. The engagement with the author is another form of professional development. One example of this type of publication is *Academic Advising Today* (*AAT*), which is a quarterly electronic publication (e-zine) of NACADA. This resource covers many types of programs in the field of academic advising. Every technique for information gathering described previously not only contributes to the planning but also offers a lens on the type of training the implementation and launch staff will need. The next step is delivering the training the team and staff need.

Training—What to Deliver

The research accomplished through viewing events, talking to providers and participants, and reading current literature results in understanding training needs. For the purposes of this chapter, training needs are categorized as physical tasks to deliver the program and development of content knowledge necessary to achieve the program goal and the institutional mission. The content required in each category is very different. Each program coordinator should evaluate the training needs for the team, since this will vary from program to program.

The knowledge for accomplishing physical tasks to deliver a program emerge very quickly as the program coordinator talks to colleagues who have delivered similar programs and the team observes a program in action. As you think about launching a one day event, understanding of the program goal is important. It frames the event and is important for fast decision-making on the day of the event. Other training needs might include

- layout of the venue,
- photos of visitors, such as the campus president or a donor for the program,
- strategies for talking to vendors,
- how to use special equipment or software,

- the importance of food options for all participants' comfort and safety,
- sustainability initiatives incorporated into the program,
- administering surveys for program assessment,
- interacting with participants and guests, and
- official kick-off or welcome activities.

This list is a good start for knowledge that your team might need to acquire before the launch of the program. We offer a relevant tip at this point to the program coordinator. Do not assume anything. For example, don't assume that team members and launch day crew know how to use a service elevator, understand the goal of program assessment, or can identify the keynote speaker. It is important to explore surface information for the implementation and launch stages and then look one layer deeper for a productive and safe experience among all who attend the event or engage with the service. In addition to physical tasks, many services require specific knowledge of content in a field.

Often a new program has a specific goal and draws upon expertise in a student affairs or academic affairs field. This category of training is referred to as development of content knowledge necessary to accomplish the program goal and contribute to the institutional mission. Knowledge of a field, student population, and/or specific technique in practice requires initial training and often ongoing development. Thus, it is important to include this key program component as you build the plan. Because it often draws from other sources such as professional organizations, it should be a budget item due to travel and conference costs. Also, it is ongoing due to knowledge generation in the field, new information on student populations, and refinement of delivery techniques. Once you have identified the content for training, developing a plan to deliver the content and knowledge is important.

Training—How to Deliver

The type of training, physical task, or content knowledge is significant when identifying how to deliver the information. All programs have certain physical tasks. Thus, it is important for the program coordinator to consider this detail and develop a comprehensive list. Often, the training for competence in completing these tasks is local and rather quick. Thus, a comprehensive list offers an opportunity to address all at one time with the team and it should be built into the worksheet for the implementing event (see Figure 7.4).

As the program coordinator builds training for competency in tasks such as using the service elevator in the student union or instructions for contacting campus security, it is important to reach out to authorities in these areas

Figure 7.4. Training activities on implementation worksheet for major fair.

	A	B	C	D	E	F
1	**Major Fair—October 15 (Implementing)**					
2	Team: Dayan (Chair), Luis, David, Kim, and Michelle					
3	Activity	Deadline	Assigned to	Cost	Note	Complete
4	Decorations **order balloons	Sept. 1	Luis	$ 100.00		Yes
5	Walk through venue and discuss layout	Sept. 15	Team	$ 100.00	Lunch for team at meeting to discuss tasks and assignments	Yes
6	Training developed by Dayan for all teams	Oct. 1	Dayan & David	$ 100.00	Breakfast & training for 2 hrs.	
7	Market to students—social media	Continuous	Michelle		Run a new post twice a day on each platform	

for materials to share with staff. Sometimes you might want to invite them to join the training for a limited amount of time. As noted in a previous section on growing the training tasks, the team might observe the actual event or service. Observations are a tool for partial or full training of the team. After observation experiences, the program coordinator can engage the team in a discussion on what training is still needed for the local program implementation. This strategy creates buy-in and certain team members can take responsibility for organizing training topics and sessions for the larger group.

The other area of training that the program coordinator must consider is content knowledge needed by staff for a new program. Whether an event or an ongoing service, the staff might require knowledge of a field (e.g., academic advising), a theory or model (e.g., culturally engaging campus environments), a student population (e.g., posttraditional students), or a technique (e.g., appreciative advising). Three strategies to facilitate acquisition of knowledge are local experts, national organizations, and scholarly literature.

We recommend investigating opportunities in your local area. Local experts are practitioners and faculty on your campus or experts in your larger community. The practitioner will focus the training experience through actual practice, with hands-on activities. The faculty facilitator will draw from their research agenda as well as other literature to create understanding. Both sources will create a learning environment close to home and serve as ongoing resources as questions emerge for the staff delivering the new program. Often, the local experts are involved on the national level through professional organizations and consulting services.

Professional organizations in student affairs and academic affairs offer a plethora of opportunities for staff and faculty to grow and develop as they launch new programs and maintain current resources and services. Some program coordinators will engage early with these resources due to the breadth and depth that can be obtained in a short period of time. For example, if the campus has committed to launching a food pantry, the annual NASPA conference would cover information on the topic as well as administrative tasks. This conference would offer a variety of sessions on food insecurity programs and students experiencing food insecurity. In addition, the conference would include sessions on evaluation and assessment of programs, hiring and developing staff, and technology tools that enhance the work environment. There are a variety of annual conferences sponsored by various professional organizations that offer an opportunity to develop understanding across a variety of issues and skill sets. The savvy program coordinator will invite other team members to attend and then develop a strategy among the group to attend as many sessions as possible across the team for maximum benefit in obtaining information and knowledge. But don't stop when the conference is over. The team should develop sessions at the home campus to synthesize what they have learned and create intentional activities to share with other team members as well as the larger community.

Another source of knowledge and information for training and development emerges from publications such as books and scholarly articles, as well as virtual tools. In the day of Google and Amazon, a quick search will offer a variety of resources on the topic. Also, the program coordinator should ask practitioners and faculty familiar with the content area of the program to point out appropriate resources that the staff could read. The activity of creating a book/article discussion group offers a richer understanding of the content and engages the team deeper into the content area. In addition to practitioners and faculty, the campus library staff are experts in finding written materials on specific topics that you can use for training and development. Today, most materials are available in virtual formats such as PDF files and videos, which allow them to be housed in a common location for universal access. This might be the campus learning management system or a cloud storage device with password protected security.

As this chapter explains, the implementation and launch stages of the IMPD depend on the human factor for delivery. At this point, the program spreadsheet has focused on tasks and assignments to identify the knowledge needed to deliver the program. This knowledge might focus on accomplishing a physical task or require deep understanding for program delivery that complements the institutional mission. It is time to move the planning process to a discussion on the art of delegating responsibility through assigning tasks for an effective work flow.

The Art of Delegation in Implementing and Launching a Program

The spreadsheet and its multiple worksheets create a story that is rich in detail. They also communicate the complexity of program development to anyone who reviews them. One person, often the author of the spreadsheet, who needs to learn a key skill based on the number of tasks outlined in the spreadsheet is the program coordinator. The story of planning, implementing, and launching a program is rarely achieved by one solo actor. Thus, it is critical that the program coordinator understand the art of delegation.

Merriam-Webster (n.d.a) defines *delegation* as "the act of empowering to act for another." Thus, the program coordinator as well as other team members must gain competency and comfort in assigning tasks to others and giving them authority to accomplish the task. What does this involve? First, the team has to be honest about each member's skill sets. Once this is clear, the second step is to assign the task to the appropriate person with clear expectations of what must be accomplished and when it must happen to support delivering the program. Third, be clear that the assignment comes with authority to move forward on behalf of the team, and trust in the team member's technique to complete the task. Fourth, the program coordinator must accept that there are many ways to accomplish most tasks and assignments, and the team member might use a strategy or technique that differs from the coordinator's expectations. If the task is accomplished at the desired level of competency and on time, the program coordinator should show appreciation and update the worksheet. Through delegation, team members take ownership and pride in the program through their contributions.

The program coordinator has many tools to guarantee task completion and competency without micromanaging each person as they focus on an assigned task. Let's talk about a few of these tools. One key component for gaining comfort with delegation is the team meeting. The spreadsheet with tasks and assignments should be reviewed at each meeting to establish expectations and address updates. Also, the program coordinator can model through a task assignment how communication occurs to celebrate accomplishments and address challenges by using the group to find solutions. If team members observe the coordinator sharing challenges and asking for assistance, team members will see the team meeting environment as safe for identifying solutions that deliver the program. This strategy moves the power from one person to members of the team and gives everyone voice on achieving program delivery. It becomes a collaboration.

Another tool is a regularly scheduled individual meeting with team members during the planning, monitoring, and implementation stages of the program. These meetings can be concise and the agenda driven to provide the program coordinator and the staff member access to each other to talk about assignments. Finally, a visual tool such as a calendar allows the program coordinator an opportunity to quickly check on task completion and check in with staff. The use of delegation in delivering and launching a new program on time is paramount. At this point, the chapter has covered key elements of the program development for the implementation and launch stages of the program. Let's talk further about the launch and what occurs after the launch.

Launching the Program

The day has arrived for the program to launch. It might be a one-time event like a conference, virtual workshop series, or career fair; it also might be a service that will offer continuous delivery to a particular population. Regardless of the type of program, the program coordinator will depend on a team using spreadsheets, relationships, and content knowledge to launch. Here are a few tips as the program is being rolled out for the campus and community.

The team is very important to early program success and long-term program fidelity. We encourage you (program coordinator) to support and nurture the team members. For example, immediately before the launch, take a few minutes to communicate enthusiasm for the accomplishments of the team and appreciation for the energy and expertise they have brought to the project. These statements might occur in an in-person meeting, through a well-crafted email, or an announcement or video on the learning management system. This effort by the program coordinator creates excitement for the launch day if it is authentic and sincere.

The worksheet for launch day is important. It clearly addresses the time element of program development by communicating what needs to occur and when it will happen. Similar to a Broadway show with a choreographed dance, it is important that everyone knows the timing of their moves for harmony and success as the program is launched. The "Launch Event" worksheet is focused on the exact day of the launch. It communicates specific tasks, who is responsible for each task, and what time the task begins. Figure 7.3, located earlier in this chapter, shares an example of this worksheet for a major fair.

As was mentioned previously in this chapter, a comprehensive planning process is appreciated most as unexpected events emerge on launch day. Team members might be ill, doors are locked that should be open, and presidents are unexpectedly called to regents or board meetings—not available to cut the ribbon. Due to the planning process that has produced a comprehensive set of worksheets, the team will overcome most obstacles for program success. And one final tip for the program coordinator and the team. Keep smiling and be positive as the launch occurs. As one of the authors experienced as she led a team planning a national conference, only the team knows when something goes wrong. A smile precludes participants from knowing the sudden twists and turns, keeps the event or service right on schedule for delivery, and accomplishes the goal. The planning team will laugh and possibly develop a strong sense of community as they reflect on these unexpected events during the program reflection stage of the model.

Moving From Launch Stage to Reflection Stage

The final chapter outlines in detail the program reflection stage, but there are a few elements of this stage that you should organize before the program launch happens. One key element to program development in the reflection stage is an exit meeting to review the event. It offers an opportunity for the team to reflect on the event as they consider the future of the event or service. It is recommended that the review occur immediately following the event; team members will have better recall on the launch tasks. If a meeting within a week after the event is not possible, ask the team members to write a reflection of the event that will be useful when the team reconvenes. This can also be set up as a discussion post on the learning management system or a document to which all contribute in the virtual environment. At the actual meeting, use the time to systematically review the worksheets for each phase of the program. Replicate the worksheets for the next iteration of the event and add the suggestions for change to this new set of documents. At some point, the program coordinator will adjust dates based on program delivery. Even if the program launched is a service that will not launch again, take the time to review the launch with the team. It creates a collaborative environment, continues team interest in the new service, and offers strategies that might be significant for implementing other programs and services. Figure 7.5 offers a worksheet for the program reflection stage for a major fair.

Celebrating a Successful Program Implementation

One final step that should be built into the program reflection after launch is to celebrate success. A new program is a change to the current status quo on

Figure 7.5. Activities on reflection worksheet for major fair.

	A	B	C	D	E	F
1	**Major Fair—October 15 (Reflecting)**					
2	**Team: Dayan (Chair), Luis, David, Kim, and Michelle**					
3	**Activity**	**Deadline**	**Assigned to**	**Cost**	**Notes**	**Complete**
4	Schedule an exit meeting with food	Oct. 16	Dayan	$ 75.00		
5	Discuss evaluation of program	Oct. 16	Dayan			
6	Discuss what needs to change	Oct. 16	Dayan		Luis will take notes	
7	Discuss volunteers for future events	Oct. 20	David		David will collect names	
8	Changes to budget	Oct. 20	David		David will collect items	
9	Update worksheets for next year's event	Oct. 30	Dayan			
10	First team meeting for next major fair	Feb. 1	Kim			
11	Reserve venue	Oct. 30	Michelle		Need to do ASAP since venue fills quickly	

| Planning & Monitoring | Implementing | Launching | Reflecting |

any campus. The process and product of change will be met with a variety of responses. It is important that the program coordinator prepares the team for these responses. One tool is to spend some time as a group reading and discussing literature on change. John Kotter (2005) has studied and written about deliberate change in society. Through his research, he has developed "The Eight-Stage Process of Creating Major Change." Even though all stages of the theory have application to most programs, "Stage 6—Generating Short-Term Wins" is especially relevant. This stage encourages celebration as certain milestones are met by individuals and the team. The act of recognizing and celebrating steps toward delivering the program builds the team and is visibly encouraging for the rest of the campus to observe.

Celebration can take on many forms and currently you probably use these types of activities for your students, faculty, and staff. Celebration can take the form of a group activity such as lunch during a meeting, a trip to the local public garden, or a group painting adventure. The act of acknowledging people at meetings for specific tasks is also important and might include a personal thank-you note and a gift card. Regardless of the action or activity, it is important that people know why the activity or the acknowledgment is occurring. It makes people feel valued and encourages them to take initiative just like Jeff did in the vignette by recommending the purchase of a broom. These activities are part of celebrating small and big wins as the program goes through the stages of planning, implementation, and launching.

Conclusion

This chapter has focused on implementing and launching the program. The opening vignette offered a short account of how details, such as a broom, emerge through the process that the program coordinator must address and incorporate into the planning and implementation stages. The tasks for these two stages of the IMPD are developed through a variety of techniques and documented on worksheets in the master spreadsheet. In addition to organizing the tasks for implementation and launch, the chapter also focused on anticipating the unexpected, training and developing the team and staff who support the program, effectively delegating tasks, and reviewing the launch of the program to prepare for future iterations of the event or providing the service daily to the campus community. The chapter reinforces a team approach that includes a postlaunch review and activities for celebrating success as a team, which are part of the reflection stage that is discussed further in chapter 9. Throughout the chapter, examples of worksheets were presented for a visual image of the process. One of the final steps after any program is launched is evaluation and assessment of the program to identify if it is achieving the stated goals. Evaluation and assessment bridges the many stages of the IMPD and informs the reflection stage. This topic is the focus of the next chapter.

8

ASSESSMENT OF
THE PROGRAM

After reading this chapter, you will be able to do the following:

1. Explain the relationship of goals, objectives, and learning outcomes to program assessment
2. Match assessment approaches to goals, objectives, and learning outcomes
3. Explain how to use assessment results to improve programs

Was the program successful? How could the program be improved? These are questions that assessment can help to answer. Assessment has been labeled "an essential dimension of student affairs practice" (Schuh, 2009, p. 1). Assessment, evaluation, and research (AER) has been identified as a professional competency for student affairs professionals. The professional competencies emphasize that student affairs professionals are to be able to use the results of assessment to inform practice (ACPA & NASPA, 2015).

Just a quick note on vocabulary. Some authors use *assessment* and *evaluation* almost interchangeably. Other authors view *assessment* as the gathering of information and *evaluation* as using that information to make decisions (Suskie, 2018). Gansemer-Topf and Kennedy-Phillips (2017) have suggested that we as program planners not get overly concerned with the distinctions. You will notice, however, as you move through this chapter that authors whom we cite will sometimes use the term *assessment* and others the term *evaluation* to mean more or less the same thing.

Too often in student affairs and higher education, the evaluation of programs is limited to an assessment of participants' satisfaction with the program—for example, "On a scale of 1 to 10, how much did you enjoy this program?" or "How likely are you to recommend this program to a friend?" Satisfaction data are important, but they are limited in how they can inform the program coordinator. As Bresciani (2009) pointed out, using satisfaction data "rarely provides information that can meaningfully identify what is 'wrong' if a student is unsatisfied" (p. 531). Furthermore, satisfaction evaluation does not let us know what, if anything, was learned or whether the goals of the program were accomplished. Clearly, there is more to be assessed than satisfaction.

One benefit of properly written objectives and learning outcomes (see chapter 4) during the program planning step is that it makes assessment of the program considerably more straightforward. Properly written objectives and learning outcomes will have specified what was to be achieved in measurable terms. In essence, you wrote the basics of your assessment plan when you wrote your goals, objectives, and learning outcomes.

We are now at the program monitoring and program reflection stages of the IMPD. Specifically, formative assessment falls into the program monitoring stage, as do attendance data (see chapter 1). Summative assessment falls into program reflection (see Figure 8.1).

Figure 8.1. Integrated model for program development—Launch and reflection.

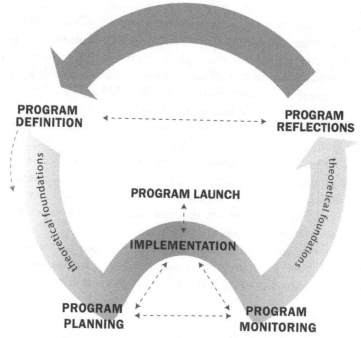

Formative and Summative Assessment

Typically, when assessment of programs is discussed, the focus is on summative assessment. However, it is beneficial to consider formative assessment as well. Both forms of assessment have important contributions to make in program development.

Formative assessment is assessment that is done about the program while the program is happening. It can be likened to tasting a dish and making adjustments while you are cooking it (e.g., "Needs more salt"). You use what you learn from formative assessment immediately to adjust the program to improve it (add salt). If you have programming experience, you probably have engaged in formative assessment without calling it that. For example, when teaching, we often find it necessary to "edit" our lesson plan during class because discussions or activities are running longer (or shorter) than planned or students simply are not understanding the material. So, too, might you find it necessary to adjust as you see things going more slowly (or more quickly) than you had planned. You also might see that the instructions you have provided for an activity are confusing or need clarification. In that case you might bring the activity to a brief halt to clarify the instructions. Or, seeing that an activity simply is not working, you could jump in with an alternative activity. These adjustments that you make on the fly are adjustments that you based on your ongoing formative assessment.

Summative assessment can be likened to getting feedback after the dish has been served and eaten, such as judges give to competitors on cooking competition programs like *Chopped* (e.g., "Needed a sauce to tie the dish together"; "Could have used just a little bit of acid"). You use summative assessment to improve the program for the future as you would use feedback to improve the dish the next time you prepare it. Summative assessment, which is the primary focus of this chapter, is part of the quality improvement/quality enhancement process. Summative assessment can inform decisions to expand or to terminate a program (Ryder & Kimball, 2015).

Satisfaction

Although the importance of satisfaction assessment is frequently dismissed or denigrated in comparison to outcomes assessment, satisfaction assessment can be valuable. Participants who were dissatisfied with a program or service are unlikely to attend another program or use another service offered by your unit or encourage others to do so. Satisfaction assessment can provide useful information for program improvement as it indicates areas for improvement (timing, location, food, length of program, presenter quality, etc.). Satisfaction assessment can provide insight into the match between what students expected and what they experienced, which has implica-tions for how the program is marketed, as well as implications for content. Assessment of satisfaction can be particularly helpful in examining whether you are meeting customer service goals. Satisfaction assessment is relatively easy and can be brief. Common examples are the feedback cards you might get at a restaurant or hotel or the quick follow-up survey from IT about how your latest ticket was handled.

Attendance/Usage

Earlier in this book, we discussed using attendance/usage information as a source of data in a needs assessment. Similarly, it is useful to examine attend-ance/usage as part of assessing the current program. Larger turnout than anticipated is an indication that you are addressing students' needs; it also indicates that you may need to scale the program up, perhaps by increasing the number/frequency of offerings, the capacity of the program at each offer-ing, or the hours of operation. Scaling up will require revisiting your budget and resources (e.g., staffing) to determine what would be needed to expand the program (see chapters 5 and 7).

Sparse attendance, however, does not necessarily indicate that the pro-gram is poor or that it does not meet students' needs. There are several fac-tors to explore related to sparse attendance. Were there other competing opportunities on the day and time of your program? Would those competing opportunities be more attractive or more compelling to your audience than your program? For example, one of us was associated with a department that scheduled its January "Welcome Back" event for Super Bowl Sunday (appar-ently, there were no football fans on the planning committee); predictably, this had a negative impact on attendance. Another issue related to scheduling of the program is the time of semester. Did you schedule your program for a particularly busy time of the semester (e.g., midterm exams, prior to a break, etc.)? Could location of the program have been a factor? Was the program scheduled in a distant, difficult-to-locate, or low-traffic location? Could relo-cating the program improve attendance? How was the program marketed? Students cannot attend programs they do not know about. All of these things should be considered when thinking about low attendance, rather than sim-ply assuming that it was a poor program.

If you have the ability to collect information about those who attended your program, you also can analyze the characteristics of those who attended compared to those who did not. Did you attract the audience you had tar-geted for this program? Are there important parts of the student body who were significantly underrepresented in attendance? This could prompt you to do some additional investigation into why certain groups did not attend.

Outcomes

Returning to your learning outcomes provides you with a clear roadmap of what to assess, if your learning outcomes were written well. Your assessment will be driven by determining whether or not students learned what you intended for them to learn. The learning outcomes will have specified when the assessment is to take place (e.g., immediately following the program, 2 weeks after the program, at the end of the semester), as well as who should be included in the assessment, what is to be assessed, and the target achievement for success.

Assessment of outcomes can be direct or indirect. Direct assessment asks students to demonstrate what they have learned (Henning & Roberts, 2016; Tucker, 2014). Indirect assessment, on the other hand, relies on self-reports of students' perceptions of their learning rather than tangible evidence of learning (Lindsay et al., 2013). For example, an indirect measure might ask students to rate on a 1-to-5 scale whether they are now more familiar with campus resources. A direct measure would ask students to list campus resources. Direct measures are viewed as stronger measures of outcomes (Henning & Roberts, 2016). Lists, short answers, true/false questions, and so on can be used as direct measures. Direct measures also can take the form of observations of the demonstration of skills, using a rubric as a measurement. This approach could be particularly useful with learning outcomes that call for students to apply or to create. Well-written learning objectives will tend to lead to direct assessment of learning.

Your assessment can take many forms. For quick, on-the-spot assessment of learning, you can employ one of many classroom assessment techniques (CATs) (Angelo & Cross, 1993). The Angelo and Cross book provides numerous examples of CATs. These include 1-minute papers, 1-sentence summaries, muddiest point, ticket out the door, and concept maps. These CATs are similar to distributing a paper evaluation form but are more focused on brief assessment of learning. You also can use classroom polling tools (such as Poll Everywhere or Kahoot) that use either clickers or students' cell phones to respond to assessment questions. Many of these can be embedded directly into slide software (such as PowerPoint or Google Slides), which can be helpful if you are using slide software in your delivery of the program. These approaches are ideal if your learning outcomes call for assessment of learning on the spot.

If your learning outcomes call for the assessment to take place as a follow-up sometime later than the program itself, you will need a different approach. First of all, to be able to do assessment sometime later (in 2 weeks, at the end of the semester, etc.), you will need to have collected contact information about your participants. If students registered for the program in advance, you can capture that information in the registration (Google Forms is one example of an easy way to do this). You also can collect such information at a check-in for the program. Your institution may have students "swipe" their IDs when they attend, which enables you to access their information (Henning & Roberts, 2016). Obviously, you will need to have planned for how you will collect information about participants prior to the program. Once you have captured their information, you can use it to send a follow-up evaluation or an invitation to an interview or focus group.

Chapter 3 discussed important considerations for various assessment methods in terms of needs assessment. Those considerations apply in assessment of program outcomes as well. Document review can play a role in your assessment if you have identified questions in a postprogram data collection (e.g., large-scale campus surveys or national surveys) that can serve as a proxy for outcomes. This approach is appropriate only if your program targeted the entire campus or if there is a way to analyze only the group of students (e.g., first-year first-generation) that your program targeted. Focus groups and interviews will give you more in-depth information from a small number of people. They also give you the opportunity to ask follow-up questions. However, interviews and focus groups can be time-consuming and may require an experienced facilitator/interviewer. Care needs to be taken to ensure that a broad range of program participants are heard from, while recognizing that you will be hearing from a small number of people. Interviews and focus groups usually involve transcription as well, adding to assessment time, and a more time-consuming analysis process as well. They do have, however, the capacity to provide compelling stories about the impact of your program that can enliven your report on the program. Just remember to ensure the anonymity of those whose stories you include. Surveys can provide you with data that are easier to compile and analyze, and they enable you to hear from more participants. The results will lend themselves to the creation of tables and graphs. A survey will not allow you to ask follow-up questions to clarify responses (although your authors have pleaded "What do you mean?" to their survey results). Students on your campus may be "surveyed out," yielding a poor response rate (see next section). It is important to craft your survey questions carefully for clarity and to keep your survey as short as possible. Do not ask for information that, although it might be nice to know, is not necessary at this stage.

Online surveys are easy to create and use with software such as SurveyMonkey, Google Forms, or Qualtrics. Such software often contains a variety of response formats (e.g., true/false, multiple choice, drop-down menus, and textboxes), as well as features such as skip logic, allowing you to "skip" the respondent to the next relevant question based on their response to a prior question. They also may have the capacity to do follow-up contacts to nonrespondents. It is likely that your institution has a license for one or more of these pieces of software. It also is true that the pace of technology change is such that there will be newer tools available to the program coordinator by the time this book is published (Henning & Roberts, 2016).

Finally, Suskie (2018) has reminded us that the scale of our assessment should match the scale of our program. "Short co-curricular experiences call for short assessments" (p. 111). Just as your needs assessment (see chapter 3) scope and scale needed to match that of your program, so should your assessment.

Survey Fatigue and Response Rates

It is important to note that, as our profession has become more focused on assessment, students are being asked to participate in more and more surveys.

> Growing emphasis on student learning and accountability has led faculty and administrators to increase assessment efforts to improve and better document the outcomes of educational programs and services. Tschepikow, Cooper, and Dean (2010) interpreted this recent upsurge in assessment activity as the arrival of an age of assessment in higher education. As assessment efforts have increased over time, so has the need to collect data for students, and many in the academy have increased the use of survey methods to do so. (Tschepikow, 2012)

However, with the increase in the number of surveys has come a large decline in response rates (Porter, 2004). Multiple surveys, particularly back-to-back surveys, appears to create "survey fatigue" and reduce response rates among college students (Porter et al., 2004). Survey nonresponse is a concern for several reasons. A very high nonresponse rate means that you could be making decisions about programs based on the feedback from a very small number of people. In addition, there may be bias in who responds and who does not, making your assessment unrepresentative. As Porter (2004) stated, "Any conclusions drawn from such unrepresentative data may be erroneous, which is problematic when such data are used for planning purposes" (p. 6).

What can be done to increase response rates? People are more likely to respond to surveys that are salient to them (Porter, 2004). Therefore, you should make it clear why your assessment is relevant to participants. ("You recently attended the Career Search Fair. Your feedback will help us to improve the program.") Multiple contacts can improve responses. This can be done in two forms: prenotification followed by the survey and the survey with one or more follow-ups (Porter, 2004).

> While they often increase costs, multiple contacts with respondents are one of the best ways to ensure a good response rate. This is one reason that Web surveys are growing in popularity: three or four contacts with respondents can be costless, while three or four paper mailings can be quite expensive, especially if postage is required. (p. 11)

Nair et al. (2008) described a follow-up process that involved telephoning nonrespondents to offer them the opportunity to complete the survey over the phone, to receive a paper copy of the survey, or to complete the survey online. They also found from the telephone conversations with nonrespondents that prenotification was indicated and adopted that practice for the next year's administration of the survey.

Another frequently used approach to increasing response rates that can be effective is to offer incentives (Porter, 2004). Preresponse incentives appear to be more effective than postresponse incentives (Gansemer-Topf & Wohlgemuth, 2009). A similar approach to incentives—offering a lottery for prizes—is also commonly used (Porter & Whitcomb, 2004); however, Porter and Whitcomb (2003, 2004) found that not only this but also the amount offered had a minimal effect on response rates. Offering a small incentive to everyone is more effective than a chance to win a bigger prize (Gansemer-Topf & Wohlgemuth, 2009). Keeping the survey short in terms of the time that it takes to respond (no more than 20 minutes is suggested) may increase response rates (Umbach, 2004). One of us recently had very strong response to a very short (three questions) Web-based survey. A "professional" looking survey also can improve response rates (Gansemer-Topf & Wohlgemuth, 2009).

With follow-up assessment, as with programming, you need to be aware of timing. Are there times in the semester when students are inundated with institutional surveys? You may want to avoid those times. Your office of institutional research or student affairs assessment will be aware of what other surveys and assessments are planned for a specific time. As we are writing, one of us is being discouraged from distributing an assessment due to two other large-scale assessments occurring on campus at the same time. The concern is avoiding oversurveying and survey fatigue (Porter et al., 2004). One suggestion for avoiding oversurveying, particularly at times when other assessment is going on, is to collaborate with one of those other efforts to include your questions as well (Wise & Barham, 2012); one of us recently added a few questions to a larger survey being distributed on campus. You also want to avoid times when you know it is likely that your survey will go unnoticed due to other demands on students (midsemester breaks, exam periods, large-scale traditional events, move-in/move-out, etc.).

Implementation Fidelity

Don't neglect examining the fidelity with which those learning strategies were delivered. *Implementation fidelity* concerns the match between what was planned and what was actually implemented (Gerstner & Finney, 2013). Implementation fidelity is also known as *program integrity* or *enacted curriculum* (Smith et al., 2017). According to Smith et al. (2017), the components of implementation fidelity include the following:

- Specific features and components of the intervention (i.e., program differentiation),
- Whether each feature or component was actually implemented (i.e., adherence),
- Quality with which features and components of the intervention were implemented,
- Perceived student responsiveness during implementation, and
- Duration of implementation. (p. 72)

If elements of the program were not delivered as planned (e.g., elements were glossed over, dropped, or changed dramatically), it is unlikely that the learning outcome would have been achieved because the program elements were designed to achieve that specific learning outcome. Although formative assessment may indicate a needed change in the plan during program execution, extensive alterations may damage implementation fidelity. Furthermore, if the elements were delivered but delivered poorly, the learning outcomes may not have been achieved. Assessment for implementation fidelity seldom occurs in student affairs (Gerstner & Finney, 2013). Gerstner and Finney suggested that changes should not be made based on outcomes assessment without an assessment of implementation fidelity. For example, if the participants did not achieve the learning outcomes and the implementation fidelity was low, the explanation may lie in the fact that participants did not receive the program as planned rather than in the program itself. If so, greater attention needs to be paid to the fidelity of program delivery before making any changes to the program itself.

Smith et al. (2017) provided a detailed description of how to conduct implementation fidelity assessment. Swain et al. (2013) suggested using an implementation fidelity checklist to assess implementation fidelity. Such a checklist would chart each program component for which there is a learning objective and then break each component down into specific features (i.e., the different things that the program presenter does). On the checklist each of the specific features is assessed by adherence, quality, and responsiveness of program participants. Swain et al. recommended that both program implementers and independent auditors complete the checklist. Then the ratings can be compared. They also suggested asking student participants to provide responsiveness information (i.e., how engaged they were).

Closing the Loop

Henning and Roberts (2016) described *assessment* as "collecting, analyzing, interpreting, and disseminating data applied for accountability and program and learning improvement" (p. 38). Suskie (2018) talked about it in terms of "closing the loop" (p. 8). Assessment, therefore, is part of the process of continuous improvement (Schuh, 2013). Once you have your assessment/ data, you need to use them to guide changes and improvements to your program. In our program development model, we have described closing the assessment loop as part of the program reflections phase. It then feeds back into the program planning phase as you plan for the next iteration of the program. Porter (2011) described her program assessment as "shining light on areas for improvement" (p. 24).

You will want to examine all of the data you have available, including attendance/usage, satisfaction, and outcomes. Earlier in this chapter we discussed possible responses to attendance and usage data. Examine your attendance usage data and consider what it might mean and how you might make adjustments to timing, location, and scale.

Satisfaction assessment can help you improve your marketing to set correct expectations for the program. Satisfaction assessment also can be used to improve customer service aspects of your program such as ease of the registration process, quality of the setting, and staffing.

Perhaps participants fell short of your learning outcomes. The program is not achieving the objectives. Assuming that implementation fidelity has been established, start by examining the learning strategies or activities that you used and look for ways to improve them to increase participant learning in those areas. Examining the assessment of the learning outcomes helps you see exactly the target areas for program improvement. Perhaps you need to devote more time to certain areas to ensure that they are learned or to emphasize the most important parts. Perhaps you need to employ less lecture and more hands-on activities. Your assessment results can guide the way to improving your program for next time.

You also should examine the assessment process itself. Look at the response rate to your assessment. Remember that a low response rate means that you may be thinking about change to the program based on the responses of very few people. If you repeat the program, you should examine your assessment plan to increase response rates. Revisit the suggestions earlier in the chapter about response rates; you also may refer to Suskie's (2018) discussion of increasing response rates. Examine your assessment instrument. Are there items that many respondents skipped? Were those items at the end of the survey? Perhaps your instrument is too long. Skipped items also could indicate that the wording was unclear, leaving respondents unsure of which option to select, or that the question touched on a sensitive area. Examining your assessment process can provide context for reporting your results and also suggestions for ways to improve your assessment plan for the future.

Using multiple data sources in assessment provides a more comprehensive assessment of the success of your program. Combining, say, satisfaction, usage, a survey measurement (or a quick CAT) of learning outcomes, and interviews with some program participants will yield a more well-rounded assessment of the program. Remember, however, to keep the scale of your assessment aligned with the scale of your program.

Reporting

As we said in chapter 1, "The program is not 'done' until all of the final reports are created, analyzed, reported, discussed, and a meeting has taken place" (p. 16, this volume). Your reporting can take many forms and can have multiple audiences. In fact, you should tailor the format and contents of your report based on your audience. Not everyone needs—or wants—to hear everything about your program.

An executive summary (one or two pages) could be shared with your vice president and other upper-level administrators (Henning & Roberts, 2016; Schuh, 2009). As Schuh observed, upper level administrators receive a large amount of material to read; "one could assert, correctly in our view, that there is an inverse relationship to the length of the documents that these people will receive and the likelihood that they will read the material" (p. 176). Your supervisor will want a more detailed, full report. You will want a comprehensive report to refer to for future iterations of the program. A PowerPoint version of your report may be a good way to share with groups such as the student affairs leadership team; such a presentation would feature your charts and graphs. Remember that large tables full of numbers are difficult for the audience to read. Consider other stakeholders, what information they might be interested in hearing, and the best format for conveying that information. Both Schuh (2009) and Henning and Roberts (2016) have provided extensive guidance for creating and presenting assessment reports.

However, don't stop with reporting the assessment results. Use them to refine and improve your program where indicated. This is an important part of the reflection stage where administrative decisions about the future of the program are made. The quality of your assessment and your assessment results play a key role in determining the future of your program.

Example

At the end of a year, the MSU Food Insecurity Committee had a number of accomplishments to look back on. Brooke Turner, director of the student union, had led the committee through their needs assessment and then helped oversee the creation of goals and objectives for the first year. The Student Activities staff, under the leadership of Ian Brown, carried out the implementation with guidance and oversight from the Food Insecurity Advisory Committee. In the fall, they focused on goals 1, 2, and 3.

1. Raise awareness on campus of food insecurity and its impacts
   a. After the Food Insecurity Awareness media campaign, 85% of students, faculty, and staff will be able to state accurately what percentage of MSU students experienced food insecurity during the past month.
   b. After attending a food insecurity workshop, participating students, faculty, and staff will be able to list three impacts that food insecurity has on student success with 80% accuracy.
2. Raise awareness of available resources for food insecure students
   a. After attending a food insecurity workshop, participants will be able to list three on- or off-campus resources that address food insecurity with 80% accuracy.
3. Establish a campus food pantry

Goal 3 had a long list of process objectives that outlined what staff would need to do to establish a campus food pantry. Ian Brown's staff and the advisory committee relied on the "Campus Food Pantry Toolkit" from the College and University Food Bank Alliance (CUFBA, 2015), which also had been helpful in the planning of the needs assessment. It turned out that establishing a campus food pantry was a complicated undertaking that involved risk management, determining and securing a location, staffing and staff training, and hundreds of small details. Refer to chapter 6 for a detailed discussion of putting the program plan together and chapter 7 for implementing the program. For the purpose of this example, we will focus on assessment under goals 1 and 3.

In terms of goal 1, after the social media campaign was completed, staff sent a brief electronic survey to faculty, staff, and students. They asked three questions that focused on if the respondent was a faculty member, a staff member, or a student; which (if any) of a list of media campaign elements (student website portal, school newspaper, daily campus e-newsletter, campus bus ads, posters, etc.) they remembered seeing; and the percentage of MSU students who experienced food insecurity in the past month according to the campaign. They sent out two email reminders "because we don't want to be annoying." Because they remembered to ask about the respondents, they were able to see that there were differences between students, faculty, and staff in terms of what media elements they recalled and in terms of ability to accurately answer the food insecurity question. Whereas faculty and staff (if they recalled the campaign) were most likely to indicate that they had seen it on the campus e-newsletter, students were more likely to report having seen it on the web portal or on campus buses. They fell short of their target, finding that only 60% of faculty, staff, and students could state the percentage of students who experienced food insecurity correctly. Students were more likely to know that percentage than were faculty and staff. After each of the food insecurity workshops, the facilitator used a classroom response system that used attendees' phones to answer the question about sources of assistance for food insecure students. Staff also examined attendance figures for the workshops, relying on an on-the-spot headcount. Attendance was disappointing to the staff; they reached a very small percentage of the campus population. However, those who did attend were able to list three sources of assistance with 87% accuracy.

In the second semester, Brown and his staff opened MSU's food pantry. They tracked the number of shoppers via headcounts and used that information to track peak times of usage. In the third month of operation, they put invitations to an interview about the shopper's experience using the food pantry on the counter in the food pantry. The invitation provided a link to sign up for an interview slot. The brief interview protocol focused on shopper satisfaction with the food pantry.

The staff prepared a number of reports, including an executive summary for President Jackson and Vice President Bruce; a longer, more detailed report for the advisory committee; and a comprehensive report for themselves.

Bruce asked for additional details and invited Ian Brown and Brooke Turner to make an 8-minute presentation to the student affairs leadership team.

The staff and the advisory committee reflected on the results of the assessment. Overall, food pantry shoppers were satisfied but expressed a desire for more evening hours and more variety in pantry offerings. Usage data supported the popularity of evening hours and also showed that early mornings tended to experience very light usage. They decided to alter the hours accordingly. To try to address the desire for more variety, staff prepared a list of desired items to post to their website and to distribute to offices and student organizations that want to sponsor food drives. They also decided to continue the media campaign approach to continue to raise awareness but to focus on those elements that had been most successful. The low attendance at educational events was disappointing, but they were not sure how to explain it. They considered dropping the educational programming approach in favor of more passive programming such as the media campaign and table tenting, as well as brief educational videos on their website.

As the example from MSU communicates, assessment is a key component for the reflection stage and impacts future iterations of the program. It is important to begin building your assessment in the program definition stage and continue to revisit it in the planning and monitoring stages. The program reflection stage offers the program coordinator and program planning team an opportunity to understand what has been achieved due to assessment results and use these results as the future of the program is discussed by the campus. The next chapter will offer further understanding of the reflection stage of the IMPD.

REFLECTIONS FORWARD

After reading this chapter, you will be able to do the following:

1. Relate the full use of the IMPD to practice
2. Apply all aspects of the model to the many programs in the field
3. Support students in their role as program developers

As we pull everything together, we are reminded that the heart of program development is the people. All of this creativity, implementation, delivery, and steps along the way are not possible without people making it happen and the people we are targeting our efforts. Leadership, respect, and skills are needed to work with all of these groups. Program administration is a constant application of challenge and support (Sanford, 1967). It has the challenges of self-management and perseverance, where one has to step into a role of a leader and a manager. At times we might think, "I just want to make a great program," without realizing all of the self-determining factors. Program development is a test of your self-efficacy (Bandura, 1997), while at the same time improving and expanding your own self-efficacy. The challenges of the self will expand and enlighten your ability to develop more complex programs as well as programs for larger and larger audiences. Think back, reflect if you will, to that first program that was inspired by you; proposed by you; designed, planned, implemented, launched, and completed . . . all by you. Think of the things that were seemingly overwhelming at the time. It is probably hard to think about those programs and those struggles now, because you are in a different place. As your skills and implicit knowledge as a programmer expanded, so did your programs. Those things that were seen as blind spots and "if I had only known" moments of clarity are now commonplace and come to you as part of the natural course of action in planning a program. Newer programming professionals may comment on your flashes of brilliance at times, but to you they are seen as a lot of hard work, trials, testing, and hoping "this will all come together." All of this is part of the suppositions of Kolb's experiential learning theory. This theory posits that there is no new learning; it is all about relearning (Kolb, 2015). That is not to say we do not learn "new" things. We definitely learn new things all of the time; that is how our brain works (Zull, 2002); it is called *plasticity*. The new things we learn are based on reflecting back to what we knew before. We make meaning out of today's program based on the experience we had with a similar program or situation in the past, recognizing certain signatures, even without consciously realizing it sometimes. By this we mean that you may reuse certain elements in your programs without realizing it. This is not a bad thing; it is just something to reflect on and see if it is true. You might also notice a similarity between developing skills for program development based on your continuous engagement with programs and the cyclical nature found in the IMPD. This learning through practice will have ongoing impact.

In addition to gaining depth and breadth to your skills, you are learning new things, and your leadership is expanding all of the time. As the program coordinator it is very easy to be focused on what we are trying to create, teach, guide, and mentor, while at the same time not being able to maintain a sense of self through reflection. This is where the support for the self comes into play. What keeps you motivated and helps you keep your energy to make more programs, or work with one more campus committee to make something great happen? What helps to keep you motivated to be the mentor and the guide those students want, need, and deserve? As we said earlier, staff, students, and committee members want you to help them, but they also want you to let them make some mistakes. It is how they build their capacity and their self-efficacy. You just provide a safety net to help them with boundaries and guidance. If your answer to the "Where do you get your support and motivation?" question is that you just love students and you get your motivation from their success, that is all well and good, but your support of yourself needs to be a bit deeper and, to be honest, a bit more self-centered. What happens to your support when you find yourself saying, "This year's group of students just didn't connect with me." We are not saying "not" to be student-centered; we are helping you to not be student-reliant.

Challenge and Supporting Others

The things we focus on in student affairs are the challenges we face and the support we provide to others—specifically, our students. This challenge and support approach works at a more global level as well. We just spent a good amount of time here looking at the theory of challenge and support from a self-reflection point of view. It is good to do that from time to time. Now we turn our attention to the challenge and support we give to those we develop programs for when we are the program coordinator as well as when we are teaching, mentoring, and guiding others as the coordinator. Make no mistake; you are the program coordinator in either role. It is you who has to make everything come together and you are the one who the vice president will look to for questions, answers, and direction when things seem to be headed toward a "plan B." As we have pointed out, the management and leadership of programming is a task that many in our field take for granted. This specialized skill set is honed and fashioned with practice—and most likely, repetition. We have heard it said that "practice makes perfect." Let's revise that a little here; perfect practice makes perfect and bad practices make for bad habits and shortcuts. By using the IMPD, we know that you will have a guide and system that will help you with every aspect of the program development stages.

When you are the chair of a committee developing a program, you have to be ready to challenge others to contribute, follow through, and remain dedicated to program development. The larger the program, the longer the preparation, planning, and development time—leading to greater difficulty in keeping participants engaged and on task. Faraway deadlines make it hard to create a sense of urgency. The program coordinator needs to challenge those on the team to keep on moving forward. This includes helping them see the bigger picture and where the program needs to end up. You should challenge students to push themselves a bit further than they think they can go. We know how to read our students, and we can see potential in them that sometimes they may not see for themselves. We need to help them test their ability and expand self-efficacy; it is what challenge is all about. Let us step back to working with colleagues for a second while we are on this particular topic. When you are the program administrator leading a group of professionals, or a mixed group of professionals and students, you need to take hold of your leadership qualities. Be that leader who is there to challenge all who work with you on programming to expand their abilities and push themselves to make things happen. This is what we mean by challenge, and it is what we mean by leadership. With leadership comes another important aspect—and that is support.

If we just "hand them the binder" and tell them everything is in there so just follow the steps and your job will be really easy, then we are not really fulfilling the support role. Sure, we handed them previous plans and things that worked or did not work. On the support side of our theory, this is not very respectful to the colleague nor the student with whom you are working.

Depending on the person this could be seen in a few ways: (a) this leader does not trust my ability so they just want me to do what last year's chair did; (b) the chair is not interested so let's just make this happen and last year was good enough; or (c) this is not really delegating; it is more just assigning so I am just doing and not contributing. There are probably many scenarios or thought processes that could fit in this example. The bottom line here is that you, as the administrative lead on the program, need to understand the talents, strengths, attitudes, and beliefs of those on your team. Support is when you take an interest in the overall program and the contributions your colleagues and students will make to the overall success for everyone involved. This binder example could also be too much support in that you have given them everything to do. You may just be trying to be helpful, and possibly a bit controlling. This too-much-support example could have a negative effect on the challenge side of our theory. Because you have done everything, there is no challenge. No challenge means your program teammates may not see their value or just lose interest in "your" program.

The flip side of too much support is not enough support. If we assign someone a job and we have every belief that they can do it, that is great. You might even tell them that along the way. You may be thinking you want to be helpful and stay out of their way so they can feel the freedom to create. In your head this might be a good thing, and your meanings are intentional and positive. This could be seen by your colleague or your student as abandonment or just getting them out of the way. You wanted them to get back to you when they were ready. Sometimes the people that we work with will tell us they are "good to go" and "they got this," but they may not have the courage or the confidence to ask those clarifying questions. In the frenzy to build programs, and quite often this has to happen in a short time frame, we might forget to check in with them or follow up. Program development is a constant surveillance type of activity. Depending on the size of the program and the proximity to the launch, you may want to have weekly or daily check-ins to make sure things are happening. This check-in with your committee will help you as the program coordinator stay on top of the system and stages of program development. It will also routinize those check-ins with people who may not be fully sure of what you are trying to do, or they do not quite have the big picture. It could also help to build in the amount of support that some of your colleagues and students will need.

Challenge and support is a lot more than just a fallback cliché when we are talking about college student development theory. As we have seen here, we can turn challenge and support inward to look at ourselves and appreciate what we are doing and learning, as well as how we are supporting our own psyche and growth. Challenge and support is how we form a team, create momentum, build capacity, and make a program come to life. This will happen at each and every step of the way on the IMPD from the recruitment email for the committee to the final reflections after the fact. Remember your program coordinator role as manager, and more importantly as the leader.

The Program Development Model Reprise

The early stages of the IMPD is where we tend to focus. That is where the action is, and where the energy of investment is generally focused. This part of the model is where potential, kinetic energy, and synthesis all come together. We will address the top right side of the model here for a moment. This chapter is about reflections. When we are standing at the end of the model, after the launch, and we have been monitoring the whole thing and making changes along the way, we arrive at an end. It could be the final end, or it could be the end for now. Regardless, program reflection begins a distinct and important aspect of the program development cycle. Figure 9.1 shares the model as we discuss the program reflection stage further in this chapter.

Figure 9.1. Integrated model for program development—Reflection.

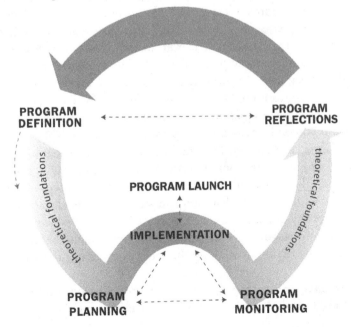

The Top Arc of the Program Development Model

Imagine that you are standing in front of a two-way mirror. Typically, these are dark pieces of glass. We can sort of see into the other side, into the other room, and notice what is going on. It is dark and a bit disconnected from the room where we are standing. We might not have the ability to hear what is going on in the other room; we can only see and speculate. The room in which we are standing may be darkened, so the mirror works better, but it is more real because we are there and part of the action. This two-way mirror analogy is what this stage of program reflection is like. At the end of the program we are in the meeting in the room with a mirror. This after-action report and meeting uses the mirror to look back over time and evaluate our program. We will return to what the two-way glass has to do with all of this in a moment.

Reflections Relate Back to Definition

That dotted line from program definition is the faded trail back to when we started all of this. Some of the things we chatted about in those initial stages will be a well-worn path, perhaps even a rut, and some of our ideas will still be there but more subtle, like an obscure trail. Finally, there are the ideas that never quite made it to the final program. They were great ideas at one point that just could not be implemented at the time of the current program. Some of these ideas need a little more infrastructure that this time frame or budget could not support. Some of the crazy brainstorming ideas we had along the way worked out perfectly. This sense of happenstance and serendipity can happen in program development as well. In some cases, our ideas were due to some constraint, financial problem, or scheduling problem that could not be avoided. Keep a list of ideas in a file to which you can return in the future. This brainstorming file could be a goldmine for the next committee as they return to the program project or even for a complementary program, the sequel if you will. Speaking of unplanned and unavoidable, there was a student-planned and student-focused program on campus that had to move into plan B and have extra communications due to the NATO summit meeting that was taking place in the same town (www.nato.int/cps/en/natolive/events_84074.htm). The student program was at a different location, but the street closures and city security created some unexpected problems. There are only so many things you can anticipate in a program, but in the end the committee has to be ready for anything. In many cases, rain is the least of your worries.

As we discussed in chapter 1, the program definition stage is when we set the budget, goals, learning outcomes, and assessment plans into motion.

This beginning definitions phase is where we would create the theoretical foundations for our program as well. All of these important details have to be established early in the program definition stage of the process so they are solid and measurable along the way and analyzed in the program reflection stage. Many of the aspects of a program can be adjusted along the way as the program rolls out from planning to implementation, and at launch. The last-minute flashes of brilliance that will streamline crowd control and catering problems can be attended to. The important things like finances, evaluations and assessments, and even travel, talent booking, and venue are vital. It is very important that the program coordinator document and make notes along the way from start to finish as well. Once you are in this room, creating reports, sending thank-you notes, and paying the bills, it may be too hard to remember some of those details.

The Other Side of the Mirror

Program reflections and a mirror make sense. We are looking back on the whole process. We are taking time to celebrate our successful program, and we are able to look at our numbers, our finances, and our statistics to see that we were able to accomplish our goals and our learning outcomes. In some cases, our program is a one-time event and the first meeting is the final meeting. No further meetings need to happen for this event. Our programs may happen on a semester/quarter basis or annually. In some cases a conference or larger program may happen every 2 years or even less frequently. Looking into the other room is how we attend to these ongoing programs. Looking back to chapter 2 we can see that many of the previous models in program development history have attended to this ongoing decision-making process (Aulepp & Delworth, 1976; Barr & Cuyjet, 1983, 1991; Cuyjet, 1996; Moore & Delworth, 1976; Saunders & Cooper, 2001). This mirror provides context and insight as well. How could we use technology to enhance the student/learner experience? What did we have to do to our program during program monitoring to make it work, to make it enjoyable, for all participants? Can we use the concepts of universal design to make future improvements to the program that seem to be "work arounds" during implementation and monitoring?

Ongoing Administrative Decisions

Jumping off from the program reflection stage, we follow the arc back to the other side to begin again next time. This arc indicates a passage of time as well. It is important that we create a detailed report (using information from our worksheets) and keep it in a safe place that can be accessed by more than one member of the committee. Student affairs is a dynamic process and industry. Many people move around and move on to other positions, campuses, and states. A great indicator of what is happening now is to look back and see what got you here. The notes that we keep and maintain now will be vital on the other side of summer and after numerous other campus programs, activities, and politics. As the coordinator it is important to build a solid team of committed and enthusiastic members. Creating a team that understands and has some history with the program is invaluable, although this may also introduce some campus politics or the notion of an in-crowd or clique on campus. All of these considerations should be examined by the coordinator and core planning team for the program. The types of notes the program coordinator may find helpful will include topics and categories like the following:

- Committee members
- Committee roles and jobs
- Frequency of committee meetings
- Budget considerations
- Alternative funding
- Sponsorships and student organization participation
- Target population to attend and whether it should be restricted or expanded
- Materials and collateral ordering, lead time, favorite vendors
- Assessment needs
- Whether the theoretical structure and grounding were appropriate for the needs
- Venue considerations and timing to reserve
- Future campus construction that may impact venue restrictions/ alternatives
- Possibility of campus partners—community engagement, service-learning, alumni/ae relations

Life on campus happens very quickly. Once the term begins it seems like a whirlwind of activity until we are suddenly at semester finals, or even spring commencement. It may seem as if everything has to happen over summer or winter breaks. These are great times to catch up on your program development checklists and worksheets to make things happen. At the same time, it is amazing what can happen between day 1 of the semester/quarter and the last day. Campus professionals and student programmers can be very productive and industrious and create a new program on the spot. It is hard to tell which came first—the campus student affairs professional or the program developer and coordinator. Which aspect of the programmer is the initial seed to making things happen? We are not sure we can answer that question. But we do know and present here the fact that using the IMPD is a vital tool for the campus administrator, student programmer, and even the faculty member who is adding experiential activities, such as internships, to their program of study. It is likely that the creator, implementer, and coordinator of the programs will use some method of program development. We found in chapter 1 that interviewing the student programming group showed their process is similar to our program development model. Here again we present our model; you will likely use a model or system by default or design. The IMPD is a design that will work.

Overall Model and Our Chapters

In the preface we introduced this book to you and outlined what you would find as you moved forward. This chapter has been a time to attend to you as the coordinator and see you as the leader and manager. We presented the challenge and support model. Leading a team through program development is akin to managing a bunch of people and advising them at the same time. So much of our work on campus is dependent on the personalities that show up to campus every day. As the coordinator or administrator (whether you are the active or adviser programmer) you can do a lot to build and foster your team. There are multiple personality and skills assessments and instruments that you can use to help build your team and understand the talents and strengths sitting around your table. We have spoken quite a lot about David Kolb's (2015) experiential learning theory. There are a few different ways you can access his work to test your committee members to determine their learning styles—for example, *How You Learn Is How You Live*, by Kay Peterson and David Kolb (2017). This book will help you, as the coordinator, understand your team better. We know from research that how we learn is typically how we teach and deliver information (Kaplan & Kies, 1995). This can help you as the coordinator in a few ways. It will help you understand who your committee members are. It could help you in how to assign jobs and roles on your committee. Finally, it can help your whole committee develop a more holistic program for your students. The more learning styles and diversity of thought on your team, the more holistic and attentive you can be to your target population.

Program Definition

Once your team is established you will be able to attend to the work of the committee and building a program. The chapters in our book that have helped with the program definition stage of the program model start with chapter 1 to explain why and how this model was developed for you as the program development coordinator. It walks you through the different stages of the whole model and was meant to help you experience the stages as much as possible. The history of program development literature in chapter 2 will help with the definition phase for some; for others, it may be something that exists, but why do we care? It is what it is, and the context helps to substantiate the model and the process. Chapter 3 on why develop this program is really about the definition stage and looking at the true need for a campus program. Many things happen on a campus and within students' lives. There are many events, concerns, and missions that could be attended to on the campus. The examination of why we look at the different ways to make an intervention or create a program is very important. This question must be answered prior to spending a lot of time, resources and energy on nonrelevant issues.

Once we decide on the "why" question, the next step would be to determine the goals and objectives of what we are really working toward, as addressed in chapter 4. We are still more in the definition stage, but this chapter starts moving us toward more actionable phases of learning outcomes and the planning stage. The money part of the program needs to have a primary emphasis; finances start with program definition but often transition into the planning stage. Chapter 5 is about the fiscal plan. At most institutions the finances and this planning have more and more importance. Financing and the money aspects have always been important, but greater scrutiny on campus, among student accounts, and within funding issues bring this point even closer to the student affairs professional. It is imperative that we act as good stewards of campus monies, student tuition dollars, and grant funding.

Program Planning

As we start to look at the goals, objectives, and the funds we start to move toward a more practical and realistic view of our programs and programming needs. The route from definition to planning is a gradual increase to the hands-on activities of planning and securing locations and materials. The roadmap and stops along the way created in the worksheets referenced in chapters 6 and 7 are important. As we establish benchmarks and check-in points, we are fully in the planning and monitoring stages of the IMPD. A constant formative evaluation is necessary here too. Those ideas and brainstorming ideas we discussed in the challenge and support sections are what happens in the planning. This is a great phase because to some degree we are developing the blue sky approach to programs. The latter parts of this section as we move toward implementation is when we have to move our idealism more toward realism. This phase is really about financial constraints, venue requirements, timing, and maybe even campus constraints or mission.

Implementation and Launch

The final stages of the IMPD turn quickly to program implementation, as outlined in chapter 7. The implementation is when we are going to print and schedule those hard-stop types of planning markers. T-shirts are being delivered, parking passes are being sent out, and participant registrations will start rolling in at any moment. The implementation phase is the prelaunch building or staging of the venue. Catering brings in the food or the refreshments and things are very real. Creating a plan of action for handling the crowds and all of the things that feel like the program has started, but it has not . . . yet. The launch is the proverbial liftoff. It is when the doors open and the first person walks into your space. The program is now "live."

Program Monitoring

We place assessment information close to the end of the book (in chapter 8) after the launch stage. This placement is where a lot of the analysis will occur, but it can also seem out of place. The initial work on the assessment plan has to happen at the beginning, during the definition stage. At the beginning, in definition, you are establishing your goals and objectives. The preparation to implement your assessments of student learning will need to be collected during the program monitoring stage, if this is that type of program. You will want to collect evaluations about the program as well. In many cases you can split your forms between an assessment of learning and the evaluation of the program process and the space. This is in the monitoring stage, because many times you have to ask people to complete these forms. You may need an incentive for them to complete the survey. You will also be monitoring that they have, and will, submit your evaluation forms. Your collection will be in person on paper, smart phone links, or via the web. Will you email a link or use a QR code they can scan as they exit the program space?

Finally, the last person leaves our space and we start the clean-up duties. The exhilaration, or some might call it exhaustion, of the program is still with you as you collect all of the evaluations/assessments, secure any money, and save the things you can reuse. Creating sustainable and reusable props and pieces within the program is good stewardship of money. Then we move to the program reflections stage that we have discussed here in chapter 9 and the two-way mirror analogy. Throughout each chapter we have offered a variety of examples to appeal to a broad audience and to support your learning of the concept, stage, or strategy within the model. The goal was to create a resource that explains program development in student support areas.

Closeout

This process called programming (or program development) is truly an added benefit for the students, the curriculum, and adds to the experience of learning (Kolb, 2015). Through programs student affairs contributes to the institutional mission and the overall curriculum, whether it be the curriculum or the cocurricular; we can influence moral and civic learning and student behaviors while they are with us on campus (Barr & Keating, 1985; Bryan & Mullendore, 1991; CAS, 2009; Cooper & Saunders, 2000; Cuyjet & Weitz, 2009; Hartwig, 2000; Maki, 2010). We have discussed the talent it takes to create programs, whether we brought that skill with us or we gained it through the time-honored "on-the-job training"; we bring those talents and contributions. The delivery of programs and programming is better created, implemented, and assessed through systematic program development methods, with intention and determination. This book provides a model for program development. We know these practices work. We have used these practices. We have outlined the 45-year history of program development models in our field. We have had groups explain their approach to program development, and how it aligns. Approaching anything with the end in mind and using a system is a smart way to approach any work (Covey, 2014).

While working with a campus student programming committee we asked them to talk through their programming process (Whitney et al., 2013). As they spoke about the importance of working as a team, working with their advisers, and pulling all of the components together, one student had a poignant comment. She said that putting on a program was so much more than just the day-of event or activity. She said the program is a sum total of the event and everything else. We took that simple statement and created $P = E3$ ("Programming" equals the "Event" and "Everything Else.") The IMPD shows the event "and" everything else. The event is the whole focus of the planning process, and at the same time it is program launch. Everything else is covered in all of the pages of this book. Program development is fun! Program development is rewarding. Program development is how we can make an impact and a difference with our students, staff, and faculty through action, activity, and demonstration. These programs make the learning and the experience a reality. Programming and programs is where theory becomes practice, and where practice is informed by theory. We are doing both, and at the same time. Program development is experiential learning for the program coordinator in real time; it better prepares you for the next program. So perhaps the IMPD is the foundation for your next great program. After all, there is no new learning; it is all about the relearning and the increasing complexity of the next best thing (Kolb, 2015).

Tasks needed 6 to 12 months prior to event/program	Assigned To	Date Assigned	Date Needed	Date Completed
Define purpose of the program				
Choose event/program/program				
Determine if committee is representative of students/participants				
Research/recruit chair				
Identify theoretical approach that supports the purpose of the program				
Draft initial learning outcomes				
Determine assessment and evaluation plan				
Explore potential sites				
Determine if sites are fully accessible to all participants				
Determine rain plan possibilities for potential sites				
Determine entry and exit points for possible sites				
Research/hire event/program/ program manager				
Determine partnering programs/ departments/colleges				
Determine student body representation—committee members, student chair, etc.				
Form committees				
Draft preliminary budgets				
Create contact lists with department members, phone numbers, email addresses				

Tasks needed 6 to 12 months prior to event/program	Assigned To	Date Assigned	Date Needed	Date Completed
Select venue				
Estimate costs/seek bids (for site charges, food, lights, equipment)				
Locate funding sources: Department budgets, division, institutional partners, NCAA, grants, private donors				
Contact institutional development office to determine rules for contacting private donors.				
Seek music referrals/auditions				
Bid music and entertainment				
Bid decorating costs				
Bid printing costs				
Seek bids on other needs				
Arrange photography (for advance shots and event/program/program)				
Determine your technology needs—websites, existing applications				
Identify social media and existing online resources available				
Design invitation/anouncements (in house or bid it out)				
Are additional languages required in printing/invitations				
Draft the Bill of Materials (BOM) that may need to purchased				
Secure permits/insurance				
Finalize budgets				
Appoint budget manager				
Research/name honorees and VIPs				

Tasks needed 6 to 12 months prior to event/program	Assigned To	Date Assigned	Date Needed	Date Completed
Compile mailing list				
Compile email list				
Estimate total number of guests				
Check date for conflicts and finalise				
Get written contracts for food, talent, site, etc. (May require working with purchasing department of the institution)				
Verify the limitations (campus rules) for catering and food at the event/ program. Are you required to use campus catering? If cosponsored by student organization do the rules change?				
Assess available upfront funding				
Procure alternate site (if event/program is outdoors)				
Plan pre-event/program				
Invite/confirm VIPs and honorees				
Identify items and possible sources for underwriting				
Order "Hold-the-Date" cards				
Set publicity schedule				
Compile media list (work with institutional departments and/or procedures)				
Draft news release, calender listings, email alerts				
Set schedule for release of media information, email alerts				
Research special permits needs, insurance, etc.				
Get bios/info on VIPs and others				

Tasks needed 3 to 6 months prior to event/program	Assigned To	Date Assigned	Date Needed	Date Completed
Set schedule for committee meetings				
Determine timeline for all social media and pre-engagement needs				
Screen #hashtags and search for unique tags for tracking				
Compile list for possible sponsors/ underwriters				
Send formal requests for underwriting/funding to major donors/corporations/sponsors				
Review designs for invitation, posters, return cards, emails				
Prepare final copy for previous items				
Consult universal design for accessiblity and program enhancements				
Prepare final copy for tickets, parking permits, etc.				
Finish mailing lists for invitations, posters, and emails				
Obtain lists of potential attendees from honourees/VIPS				
Arrange radio/TV sponsor, promos, PSAs				
Set menu				
Get written reply on celebrity participation/specific needs				
Finalize sound/lighting contract				
Select and order awards and trophies				
Tasks needed 2 months prior to event/program	Assigned To	Date Assigned	Date Needed	Date Completed
Address and stuff invitations, including personal notes				
Mail invitations				

Tasks needed 2 months prior to event/program	Assigned To	Date Assigned	Date Needed	Date Completed
Hold underwriting/preview party coinciding with mailing of invitations; invite the media				
Distribute posters				
Finalize transportation, accommodations for VIPs, honorees				
Finalize contracts for decorations, rentals				
Confirm radio/TV presence				
Send press releases for celebs, VIPs, and honorees				
Determine campus safety needs/ community emergency response needs as appropriate				
Get sponsors' corporate logos				
Determine number and location of needed signage				
All chairpersons review plans				
Hold event/program walk-through with committee chairs, staff, vendors				
Review and revise budget				
Review task assignment				
Start phone work for table sponsorships (corporate, VIP)				
Tasks needed 1 month prior to event/program	Assigned To	Date Assigned	Date Needed	Date Completed
Phone follow-up on tickets				
Place newspaper ads				
Contact news media for stories, announcements, and calender listings				
Compile contents list for VIP welcome kits				

Tasks needed 1 month prior to event/program	Assigned To	Date Assigned	Date Needed	Date Completed
Schedule rehearsals/volunteer assignments for event/program				
Confirm host/registration staff and schedule				
Assign tables/seats to confirm adequate seating				
Give caterer estimate for number of participants				
Tasks needed 2 weeks prior to event/program	Assigned To	Date Assigned	Date Needed	Date Completed
Continue phone follow-up for ticket/table sales				
Assign seats/head table, and speakers' platform				
Arrange to meet VIPs at train/airport/hotel				
Confirm all transportation (airline, bus, train, limo, car)				
Confirm lodging				
Prepare transportation and lodging checklists (flight number, airline, who meets flight, etc.)				
Confirm security for VIPs				
Prepare welcome packets for VIPs/chairs/key staff				
Schedule deliveries of equipment, rentals				
Meeet with committee chairs/vendors/staff				
Confirm setup time with site				
Finalize plans with party designer				
Meet with chair and staff for finalizing plans				

Tasks needed 1 week prior to event/ program	Assigned To	Date Assigned	Date Needed	Date Completed
Distribute day-to-day schedule leading up to day-of event				
Finish phone follow-ups for sales				
Confirm number attending				
Finish seating assignments				
Hold training session with volunteers/finalize assignments				
Name three volunteers to assist with emergencies				
Finalize registration staff				
Write out all registration procedures to give to staff for consistency				
Write out emergency plans in bulleted list form for easy reference				
Print out detailed schedule for event with staff directions				
Distribute seating chart table assignments to host				
Schedule return of rented/loaned equipment				
Reconfirm event/program site, hotel rooms, and transportation				
Finalize the catering guarantee				
Confirm printed materials are on schedule for delivery				
Finalize snacks/meals for confirmed volunteers				
Deliver final scripts				
Increase social media presence in final prep week incrase presence of your #hashtags				
Follow-up calls to news media for both advance and event/program				

Tasks needed 1 week prior to event/program	Assigned To	Date Assigned	Date Needed	Date Completed
Distribute more posters				
Hold final walk-through at site				
Hold rehearsals as needed				
Establish amount of petty cash needed for tips, emergencies				
Check or clean outfit for event/program				
Pin cashier's check for celebrity, special permits, etc. on outfit being worn to event/program				
Day before event/program	Assigned To	Date Assigned	Date Needed	Date Completed
Layout registration and establish your headquarters area				
Prepare areas with needed materials for easy set-up tomorrow				
Walk the whole event site and make a list of last minute needs				
Confirm online links, QR codes are working properly				
Organize printed material for easy distribution				
Make sure all petty cash and checks are ready				
Tasks needed day of event/program	Assigned To	Date Assigned	Date Needed	Date Completed
Arrive early to unpack and inventory supplies, etc.				
Have evaluation/assessment forms ready to distribute				
Take pictures during events, take video, ask people to post to social media				
Keep a headcount DURING the program				

Tasks needed day of event/program	Assigned To	Date Assigned	Date Needed	Date Completed
Review your last-minute needs list from yesterday				
Check for VIPs in place with scripts				
Reconfirm snacks and meal schedule for volunteers				
Check with volunteers to ensure all tasks are covered				
Set up registration area				
Check sound/light equipment and staging before rehearsal				
Review details with caterer				
Review emergency plan and campus safety involvement/placement				
Make final calls and faxes				
Greet special guests: President, VPs, deans, faculty				
Wander your venue to ensure all functions are running as planned				
Tasks needed within the week after event/program	Assigned To	Date Assigned	Date Needed	Date Completed
Send thank you notes to dignitaries				
Conduct a follow up meeting with committee(s) to discuss program				
Transcribe/input/analyze evaluation and assessment forms				
File appropriate funding reports				

REFERENCES

American College Personnel Association & National Association of Student Personnel Administrators. (2015). *Professional competency areas for student affairs practitioners.*

American Council on Education, Committee on Student Personnel Work (1937). *The student personnel point of view.* American Council on Education Studies, series 1, vol. 1, no. 3.

American Council on Education, Committee on Student Personnel Work (1949). *The student personnel point of view.* American Council on Education Studies, series 6, vol. 1, no. 13.

American Marketing Association. (2013). *Marketing.* [Definition]. https://www .ama.org/the-definition-of-marketing/

Anderson, L. W., Krathwohl, D. R., & Bloom, B. S. (2001). *A taxonomy for learning, teaching, and assessing: A revision of Bloom's taxonomy of educational objectives.* Longman.

Angelo, T., & Cross, K. (1993). *Classroom assessment techniques: A handbook for college teachers* (2nd ed.). Jossey-Bass.

Aulepp, L., & Delworth, U. (1976). *Training manual for the ecosystem model: Assessing and designing campus environments.* Western Interstate Commission for Higher Education.

Bandura, A. (1997). *Self-efficacy: The exercise of control.* Freeman.

Banning, J. H. & Kaiser, L. (1974). An ecological perspective and model for campus design. *Personnel and Guidance Journal, 52*(6), 370–375. https://doi .org/10.1002/j.2164-4918.1974.tb04043.x

Barr, M. J. (2002). *Academic administrator's guide to budgets and financial management.* Jossey-Bass.

Barr, M. J. (2016). Budgeting and fiscal management for student affairs. In G. S. McClelland, J. Stringer, and Associates (Eds.), *The handbook of student affairs administration* (4th ed., pp. 509–534). Jossey-Bass.

Barr, M. J., & Cuyjet, M. J. (1983). Program development and implementation. In T. K. Miller, R. B. Winston Jr., & Associates (Eds.), *Administration and leadership in student affairs: Actualizing student development in higher education* (pp. 447–475). Accelerated Development, Inc.

Barr, M. J., & Cuyjet, M. J. (1991). Program development and implementation. In T. K. Miller, R. B. Winston Jr., & Associates (Eds.), *Administration and leadership in student affairs: Actualizing student development in higher education* (2nd ed., pp. 707–739). Accelerated Development, Inc.

Barr, M. J., & Keating, L. A. (1985). *Developing effective student service programs: Systematic approaches for practitioners.* Jossey-Bass.

Bender, B. (2017). College and university missions: Purposes, principles, and perspective. In B. D. Ruben, R. DeLisi, and R. A. Gigliotti (Eds.), *A guide for leaders in higher education: Core concepts, competencies, and tools* (pp. 40–52). Stylus.

Bloom, B. S. & Krathwohl, D. R. (1956). *Taxonomy of educational objectives: The classification of educational goals, by a committee of college and university examiners. Handbook I: Cognitive domain.* Longman Green.

Bolman, L. G., & Deal, T. E. (2003). *Reframing organizations: Artistry, choice, and leadership.* Jossey-Bass.

Bray, N. J., & Major, C. H. (2011). Status of journals in higher education. *The Journal of Higher Education, 82*(4), 479–503. https://muse.jhu.edu/article/447042

Bresciani, M. J. (2009). Implementing assessment to improve student learning and development. In G. S. McClellan, J. Stringer, & Associates (Eds.), *The handbook of student affairs administration* (3rd ed., pp. 526–544). Jossey-Bass.

Brown, P. G. (2019). *Developing a co-curricular learning model: A compendium of blog posts on residential curriculum and curricular approaches* (3rd ed.). http://book.roompact.com

Bryan, W. A., & Mullendore, R. H. (1991). Operationalizing CAS standards for program evaluation and planning. In W. A. Bryan, R. B. Winston Jr., & T. K. Miller (Eds.), *Using professional standards in student affairs: New directions for student services* (pp. 29–44). Jossey-Bass.

Budhai, S. S. (Ed.). (2019). *Rethinking student affairs for online learners.* NASPA (Student Affairs Administrators in Higher Education).

BusinessDictionary. (n.d.). Budgeting. In *BusinessDictionary.com dictionary.* [Definition]. http://www.businessdictionary.com/definition/budgeting.html

Carroll, L. (2001/1865). *Alice's adventures in wonderland.* Lerner Publishing Group.

Chave, J. (2013). *A case study of gender neutral policies in university housing* [Doctoral dissertation, Lynn University]. ProQuest No. 3479819.

Chickering, A. W., & Reisser, L. (1993). *Education and identity* (2nd ed.). Jossey-Bass.

Claar, J., & Cuyjet, M. (2000) Program planning and implementation. In M. J. Barr, M. K. Desler, & Associates (Eds.), *The handbook of student affairs administration* (2nd ed., pp. 311–326). Jossey-Bass.

College & University Food Bank Alliance. (2015, September). *Campus food pantry toolkit.* https://sites.temple.edu/cufba/getting-started/

Cooper, D. L., & Saunders, S. A. (2000). Assessing programmatic needs. In D. L. Liddell & J. P. Lund (Eds.), *Powerful programming for student learning* (pp. 5–20). Jossey-Bass.

Cooper, R. M. (2009). Planning for and implementing data collection. In J. H. Schuh & Associates (Eds.), *Assessment methods in student affairs* (pp. 51–75). Jossey-Bass.

Council for the Advancement of Standards in Higher Education. (2009). *CAS professional standards for higher education* (7th ed.).

Council for the Advancement of Standards in Higher Education, Wells, J. B., & Henry-Darwish, N. (2019). *CAS professional standards for higher education.*

Covey, S. R. (2014). *The 7 habits of highly effective people: Powerful lessons in personal change*. Simon & Schuster.

Crawley, A. (2012). *Supporting online students: A practical guide to planning, implementing, and evaluating services*. Jossey-Bass.

Cuyjet. M. J. (1996). Program development and group advising. In S. R. Komives, D. B. Woodard Jr., & Associates (Eds.), *Student services: A handbook for the profession* (3rd ed., pp. 397–414). Jossey-Bass.

Cuyjet, M. J., & Weitz, S. (2009). Program planning and implementation. In G. S. McClellan, J. Stringer, & Associates (Eds.), *The handbook of student affairs administration* (3rd ed., pp. 545–564). Jossey-Bass.

Delworth, U., Hanson, G. R., & Associates. (1980). *Student services: A handbook for the profession*. Jossey-Bass.

Doran, G. T. (1981). There's a S.M.A.R.T. way to write management's goals and objectives. *Management Review, 70*(11), 35–36.

Drum, D. J. (1980). Understanding student development. In W. H. Morrill, J. C. Hurst, & E. R. Oetting (Eds.), Dimensions of intervention for student development (pp. 14–38). Wiley.

Drum, D. J., & Figler, H. E. (1973). *Outreach in counseling*. Intext Educational Publishers.

Dubick, J., Mathews, B., & Cady, C. (2016). *Hunger on campus: The challenge of food insecurity for college students*. https://studentsagainsthunger.org/wp-content/uploads/2016/10/Hunger_On_Campus.pdf

Evans, N. J. (1987). A framework for assisting student affairs staff in fostering moral development. *Journal of Counseling and Development, 66*(4), 191–194. https://doi.org/10.1002/j.1556-6676.1987.tb00845.x

Evans, N. J., Forney, D. S., Guido, F. M., Patton, L. D., & Renn, K. A. (2010). *Student development in college: Theory, research, and practice*. Jossey-Bass.

Gallagher, A., & Thordarson, K. (2018) *Design thinking for school leaders: Five roles and mindsets that ignite positive change*. Association for Supervision & Curriculum Development.

Gansemer-Topf, A. M., & Kennedy-Phillips, L. C. (2017). Assessment and evaluation. In J. H. Schuh, S. R. Jones, & V. Torres (Eds.), *Student services: A handbook for the profession* (6th ed., pp. 327–343). Jossey-Bass.

Gansemer-Topf, A. M., & Wohlgemuth, D. R. (2009). Selecting, sampling, and soliciting subjects. In J. H. Schuh & Associates (Eds.), *Assessment methods for student affairs* (pp. 77–105). Jossey-Bass.

Garrison, M. E. B., Pierce, S. H., Monroe, P. A., Sasser, D. D., Shaffer, A. C., & Blalock, L. B. (1999). Focus group discussions: Three examples from family and consumer science research. *Family and Consumer Science Research Journal, 27*(4), 428–450. https://doi.org/10.1177/1077727X99274004

Gerstner, J. J., & Finney, S. J. (2013). Measuring implementation fidelity of student affairs programs: A critical component of the outcomes assessment cycle. *Research and Practice in Assessment, 8*, 15–28. http://www.rpajournal.com/dev/wp-content/uploads/2013/11/SF2.pdf

Haber, P. (2006). Structure, design, and models of student leadership programs. In S. R. Komives, J. P. Dugan, J. Owen, W. Wagner, & C. Slack (Eds.), *Handbook of student leadership programs* (pp. 29–51). NCLP.

Haber, P. (2011). Formal leadership models. In S. Komives, J. P. Dugan, J. E. Owen, C. Slack, & W. Wagner (Eds.), *The handbook for student leadership development* (2nd ed., pp. 231–255). Jossey-Bass.

Harrow, A. J. (1972). *A taxonomy of the psychomotor domain: A guide for developing behavioral objectives.* David McKay.

Hart Research Associates. (2009). *Learning and assessment: Trends in undergraduate education.* American Association of Colleges and Universities. https://www.aacu.org/sites/default/files/files/LEAP/2009MemberSurvey_Part1.pdf

Hartwig, M. C. (2000). Programming: Nuts and bolts. In D. L. Liddell & J. P. Lund (Eds.), *Powerful programming for student learning* (pp. 45–56). Jossey-Bass.

Henning, G. W. (2014). Tenet two: Cultivating a culture of assessment. In K. Yousey-Elsener, E. Bentrim, & G. W. Henning (Eds.), *Coordinating student affairs divisional assessment: A practical guide* (pp. 11–34). Stylus.

Henning, G. W., & Roberts, D. (2016). *Student affairs assessment: Theory to practice.* Stylus.

Higher Education Research Institute. (n.d.). Higher Education Research Institute & Cooperative Institutional Research Program. heri.ucla.edu

Huebner, L. A., & Corazzini, J. G. (1978). Eco-Mapping: A dynamic model for intentional campus design. *Catalog of Selected Documents in Psychology, 8*(1), 9.

Hurst, J. C., & Jacobson, J. K. (1985). Theories underlying students' needs for programs. In M. Barr & L. Keating (Eds.), *Developing effective student service programs: Systematic approaches for practitioners* (pp. 113–136). Jossey-Bass.

Kaplan, E. J., & Kies, D. A. (1995). Teaching styles and learning styles: Which came first? *Journal of Instructional Psychology, 22*(1), 29–33.

Keeling, R. P., American College Personnel Association, & National Association of Student Personnel Administrators (U.S.). (2006). *Learning reconsidered 2: Implementing a campus-wide focus on the student experience.*

Keeling, R. P., Dungy, G. J., American College Personnel Association, & National Association of Student Personnel Administrators (U.S.). (2004). *Learning reconsidered: A campus-wide focus on the student experience.* ACPA.

Kerlinger, F. N. (1986). *Foundations of behavioral research* (3rd ed.). Harcourt Brace.

Keys, D. (1982). *Earth at Omega: Passage to planetization.* Branden Press.

Kolb, D. A. (2015). *Experiential learning* (2nd ed). Pearson.

Komives, S. R. (2019). Engagement with campus activities matters: Toward a new era of educationally purposeful activities. *Journal of Campus Activities Practice & Scholarship, 1,* 14–25. https://www.naca.org/JCAPS/Documents/Komives_Article_JCAPS_Issue_1.pdf

Kotter, J. (2005). *Our iceberg is melting: Changing and succeeding under any conditions.* St. Martin's Press.

Krathwohl, D. R. (2002). A revision of Bloom's taxonomy: An overview. *Theory into Practice, 41*(4), 212–218. https://www.depauw.edu/files/resources/krathwohl.pdf

Krathwohl, D. R., Bloom, B. S., & Masia, B. B. (1973). *Taxonomy of educational objectives: The classification of educational goals. Book 2: Affective domain.* David McKay.

Kuh, G. D. (1982). Purposes and principles of needs assessment in student affairs. *Journal of College Student Personnel, 23*(3), 202–209.

Kuh, G. D. (1999). A framework for understanding student affairs work. *Journal of College Student Development, 40*(5), 530–537.

Kuh, G. D. (2008). *High-impact educational practices: What they are, who has access to them, and why they matter.* Association of American Colleges and Universities.

Lasher, W. F., & Greene, D. L. (2001). College and university budgeting: What do we know? What do we need to know? In J. L. Yeager, G. M. Nelson, E. A. Potter, J. C. Weidman, & T. G. Zullo (Eds.), *ASHE reader on finance in higher education* (2nd ed., pp. 475–502). Pearson Custom Publishing.

Lee, Y. F., Altschuld, J. W., & White, J. L. (2007). Problems in needs assessment data: Discrepancy analysis. *Evaluation and Program Planning, 30*(3), 258–266. https://doi.org/10.1016/j.evalprogplan.2007.05.005

Lewis, M. D., & Lewis, J. A. (1974). A schematic for change. *Personnel and Guidance Journal, 52*(5), 320–323. https://doi.org/10.1002/j.2164-4918.1974.tb04034.x

Lexico. (n.d.). Scope. [Definition]. In *Oxford Dictionary.* https://www.lexico.com/en/definition/scope

Lindsay, N., Hourigan, A., Smist, J., & Wray, L. (2013). "Let me be direct": Using direct assessments with student leaders. *About Campus, 17*(6), 30–32. https://doi.org/10.1002/abc.21103

Lloyd-Jones, E., & Smith, M. R. (1938). *A student personnel program for higher education.* McGraw-Hill.

Maddox, D. (1999). *Budgeting for not-for-profit organizations.* Wiley.

Maki, P. L. (2010) *Assessing for learning: Building a sustainable commitment across the institution.* Stylus.

McNair, T. B., Albertine, S., Cooper, M. A., McDonald, N., & Major, T. Jr. (2016). *Becoming a student-ready college: A new culture of leadership for student success.* Jossey-Bass.

Meisinger, R. J. (1994). *College and university budgeting: An introduction for faculty and academic administrators* (2nd ed.). National Association of College and University Business Officers.

Merriam Webster. (n.d.a). Delegation. [Definition]. In *Merriam-Webster.com dictionary.* https://www.merriam-webster.com/dictionary/delegation

Merriam Webster. (n.d.b). Programming. [Definition]. In *Merriam-Webster.com dictionary.* https://www.merriam-webster.com/dictionary/programming

Miller, T. K., & Prince, J. S. (1976). *The future of student affairs.* Jossey-Bass.

Moore, M., & Delworth, U. (1976). *Training manual for student service program development.* Western Interstate Commission for Higher Education.

Morrill, W. H. (1980). Program development. In U. Delworth & G. R. Hanson (Eds.), *Student services: A handbook for the profession* (pp. 331–349). Jossey-Bass.

Morrill, W. H., Hurst, J. C., & Oetting, E. R. (1980). *Dimensions of intervention for student development*. Wiley.

Morrill, W. H., Oetting, E. R., & Hurst, J. C. (1974). Dimensions of counselor functioning. *Personnel and Guidance Journal, 52*(6), 354–359.

Mosier, R. (1989). Health and wellness programs. In J. H. Schuh (Ed.), *Educational programming in college and university residence halls* (pp. 122–138). ACUHO-I.

Nair, C. S., Adams, P., & Mertova, P. (2008). Student engagement: The key to improving survey response rates. *Quality in Higher Education, 14*(3), 225–232. https://doi.org/10.1080/13538320802507505

National Survey of Student Engagement. (2013). *Promoting high-impact practices: Pushing boundaries, raising the bar*. Indiana University Center for Postsecondary Research.

National Survey of Student Engagement. (2017). *Engagement insights: Survey findings on the quality of undergraduate education—Annual results 2017*. Indiana University Center for Postsecondary Research.

Nuss, E. M. (2003). The development of student affairs. In S. K. Komives, D. B. Woodard, & Associates (Eds.), *Student services: A handbook for the profession* (4th ed., pp. 65–88). Jossey-Bass.

Patrick, M. E., Maggs, J. L., & Osgood, D. W. (2010). LateNite Penn State alcohol-free programming: Students drink less on days they participate. *Prevention Science, 11*(2), 155–162. https://doi.org/10.1007/s11121-009-0160-y

Peterson, K., & Kolb, D. A. (2017). *How you learn is how you live: Using nine ways of learning to transform your life*. Berrett-Koehler.

Porter, M. C. (2011). Assessing alternative breaks: Moving beyond sleeping on floors and pass-the-candle reflection. *About Campus, 16*(5), 21–24. https://doi.org/10.1002/abc.20077

Porter, S. R. (2004). Raising response rates: What works? *New Directions for Institutional Research, 2004*(121), 5–21. https://doi.org/10.1002/ir.97

Porter, S. R., & Whitcomb, M. E. (2003). The impact of lottery incentives on student survey response rates. *Research in Higher Education, 44*(4), 389–407. https://doi.org/10.1023/A:1024263031800

Porter, S. R., & Whitcomb, M. E. (2004). Understanding the effect of prizes on response rates. *New Directions for Institutional Research, 2004*(121), 51–62. https://doi.org/10.1002/ir.100

Porter, S. R., Whitcomb, M. E., & Weitzer, W. H. (2004). Multiple surveys of students and survey fatigue. *New Directions for Institutional Research, 2004*(121), 63–73. https://doi.org/10.1002/ir.101

Renger, R. (2002). A three-step approach to teaching logic models. *The American Journal of Evaluation, 23*(4), 493–503. https://doi.org/10.1016/s1098-2140(02)00230-8

Roberts, D. C. (2003). Community and programming. In S. K. Komives, D. B. Woodard, & Associates (Eds.), *Student services: A handbook for the profession* (4th ed., pp. 539–554). Jossey-Bass.

Roberts, D. C. (2011). Community development. In J. H. Schuh, S. R. Jones, & S. R. Harper (Eds.), *Student services: A handbook for the profession* (5th ed., pp. 448–467). Jossey-Bass.

Roberts, D. C., & Ullom, C. (1989). Student leadership program model. *NASPA Journal, 27*(1), 67–74.

Ryder, A. J., & Kimball, E. W. (2015, Winter). Assessment as reflexive practice: A grounded model for making evidence-based decisions in student affairs. *Research & Practice in Assessment, 10*, 30–45. https://files.eric.ed.gov/fulltext/EJ1137937 .pdf

Sanford, N. (1967). *Where colleges fail: A study of the student as a person.* Jossey-Bass.

Saunders, K., & Cooper, R. M. (2009). Instrumentation. In J. H. Schuh & Associates (Eds.), *Assessment methods for student affairs* (pp. 107–139). Jossey-Bass.

Saunders, S. A., & Cooper, D. L. (2001). Programmatic interventions: Translating theory to practice. In R. B. Winston Jr., D. G. Creamer, T. K. Miller, & Associates (Eds.), *Professional student affairs administrator* (pp. 309–340). Routledge.

Schloss, P. J., & Cragg, K. M. (2013). The nature and role of the budget processes. In P. J. Schloss & K. M. Cragg (Eds.), *Organization and administration in higher education* (pp. 101–124). Routledge.

Schuh, J. H. (2009). Writing reports and conducting briefings. In J. H. Schuh & Associates (Eds.), *Assessment methods for student affairs* (pp. 171–189). Jossey-Bass.

Schuh, J. H. (2013). Developing a culture of assessment in student affairs. *New Directions for Student Services, 2013*(142), 89–98. https://doi.org/10.1002/ ss.20052

Schuh, J. H., & Triponey, V. L. (1993). Fundamentals of program design. In R. B. Winston, S. Anchors, & Associates (Eds.), *Student housing and residential life* (pp. 423–442). Jossey-Bass.

Seemiller, C. & Whitney, R. (2020). Creating a taxonomy of leadership competency development. *Journal of Leadership Education, 19*(1), 119–132.

Shutt, M. D., Garrett, J. M., Lynch, J. W., & Dean, L. A. (2012). An assessment model as best practice in student affairs. *Journal of Student Affairs Research and Practice, 49*(1), 65–82. https://doi.org/10.1.1515/jsarp-2012-6277

Smith, K. L., Finney, S. J., & Fulcher, K. H. (2017). Actionable steps for engaging assessment practitioners and faculty in implementation fidelity research. *Research & Practice in Assessment, 12,* 71–86. https://files.eric.ed.gov/fulltext/EJ1168812 .pdf

Strayhorn, T. L. (2016). An overview of relevant theories and models of practice. In G. S. McClellan, J. Stringer, & Associates (Eds.), *The handbook of student affairs administration* (4th ed., chap. 7, pp. 135–156). Jossey-Bass.

Student Government Resource Center & College and University Food Bank Alliance. (2015). *Running a campus food pantry student government toolkit.* https:// cufba_Toolkit_FINAL.pdf

Styles, M. (1985). Effective models of systematic programming planning. In M. Barr & L. Keating (Eds.), *Developing effective student service programs: Systematic approaches for practitioners* (pp. 181–202). Jossey-Bass.

Suskie, L. (2009). *Assessing student learning: A common sense guide* (2nd ed.). Jossey-Bass.

Suskie, L. (2018). *Assessing student learning: A common sense guide* (3rd ed.). Jossey-Bass.

Swain, M. S., Finney, S. J., & Gerstner, J. J. (2013). A practical approach to assessing implementation fidelity. *Assessment Update, 25*(1), 5–7, 13.

Tschepikow, W. K. (2012). Why don't our students respond? Declining participation in survey research among college students. *Journal of Student Affairs Research and Practice, 49*(4), 447–462. https://doi.org/10.1515/jsarp-2012-6333

Tucker, J. M. (2014). Stop asking students to "strongly agree": Let's directly measure cocurricular learning. *About Campus, 19*(4), 29–32. https://vcsa.ucsd.edu/_files/assessment/learning-community-mtgs/april-3_tucker-2014-about_campus_direct_measure_cocurricular_learning.pdf

Umbach, P. D. (2004). Web surveys: Best practices. *New Directions for Institutional Research, 2004*(121), 23–38. https://doi.org/10.1002/ir.98

Upcraft, M. L., & Schuh, J. H. (1996). *Assessment in student affairs: A guide for practitioners.* Jossey-Bass.

Watkins, R., Meiers, M. W., & Visser, Y. L. (2012). *A guide to assessing needs: Essential tools for collecting information, making decisions, and achieving development results.* The World Bank.

Western Interstate Commission for Higher Education. (1973). *The ecosystem model: Designing campus environments.*

Wiggins, G., & McTighe, J. (2005). *Understanding by design.* Association for Supervision & Curriculum Development.

Wise, V. L., & Barham, M. A. (2012). Assessment matters: Moving beyond surveys. *About Campus, 17*(2), 26–29. https://doi.org/10.1002/abc.21077

W. K. Kellogg Foundation. (2004). *W. K. Kellogg Foundation logic model development guide.*

Wolf, D. F. (2016). Raising friends and raising funds. In G. S. McClellan, J. Stringer & Associates (Ed.), *The handbook of student affairs administration* (pp. 581–594). Jossey-Bass.

Whitney, R., Early, S., & Whisler, T. (2016). Create a better flow through sequencing resident assistant training. *Journal of College and University Student Housing, 43*(1), 28–43.

Whitney, R., Vandermoon, T., & Mynaugh, A. (2013). Advising: The dance toward the periphery of self-discovery. *Campus Activities Programming, 46*(1), 43–45.

Zull, J. (2002). *The art of changing the brain: Enriching the practice of teaching by exploring the biology of learning.* Stylus.

ABOUT THE AUTHORS

Sharon A. Aiken-Wisniewski is a clinical professor and director for the higher education program in the Department of Educational Leadership and Policy (ELP) at the University of Utah. Her career has focused on programs and services that promote undergraduate access, retention, and goal completion in the role of practitioner, administrator, and educator. These areas include academic advising, first-year experience courses and services, orientation, peer mentoring, enrollment management services offered through a one-stop shop model, and retention technology tools. Through these areas, her experience in developing, planning, and implementing programs has evolved over a 25-year career.

In her current position, Aiken-Wisniewski teaches courses focused on student affairs and higher education, advises graduate students, serves as coeditor for the *NACADA Journal,* and is a fellow for the Excellence in Academic Advising Initiative. Her research focus is informed by her blended identities as an educator, administrator, advising practitioner, and scholar. She infuses her lived experiences with research opportunities to gain meaning and perspective. To further promote understanding of the scholar-practitioner experience, she has facilitated and participated in research teams that investigate the meaning of various components of the undergraduate experience and inform program development. Her research has focused on women's career choices, women's experiences in higher education, and academic advising as a profession. She grew up in Vermont and has a BA in political science from the University of Maine at Presque Isle, an MS in international studies from Troy State, and a PhD in educational leadership and policy from the University of Utah.

Rich Whitney is an associate professor and program director in the doctoral program in organizational leadership at the University of La Verne in Southern California. His teaching interests include leaders' consciousness of self, brain-based learning, and program development contributions to andragogy. Previously, he was a professor in the counseling/college student development program at DePaul University in Chicago. Other higher education experience includes the University of Nevada, in his hometown of Reno, in student services and as assistant director for management and leadership programs for extended studies. Whitney has been training, facilitating, and speaking to groups on leadership throughout his professional career. As a proponent of experiential learning theory, he believes that program development and curriculum complement each other creating subject matter context for the learning experience.

Over the last 20 years Whitney has acquired an extensive background in programming and program development. His experiences include higher ed and student affairs programs as well as the creation of youth camps and leadership. He worked with a team to revise a national youth leadership training program engaging learning theory and contemporary leadership practices. Most recently he created, developed, and implemented an experiential leadership development program for the 45,000 participants at the 24th World Scout Jamboree. His research, writing, speaking, and presentations include the topics of leadership, leadership development, and leadership education.

Deborah J. Taub is professor and chair of the student affairs administration department at Binghamton University. She has been a full-time faculty member in graduate professional preparation in student affairs for over 20 years; she previously taught at the University of North Carolina Greensboro and at Purdue University. She is the coeditor of two volumes in Jossey-Bass's New Directions for Student Services series: *Preventing College Student Suicide* (2013) and *Assisting Bereaved College Students* (2008). She has published over 25 book chapters and articles in peer-reviewed journals. Her research interests include psychosocial and identity development in today's college students, underrepresented and underserved populations in higher education, and graduate preparation in student affairs.

Taub is a member of the editorial board of the *Journal of Student Affairs Research and Practice*. She has been recognized frequently for her scholarship and teaching, including ACUHO-I's Research and Publication Award, NASPA's Robert H. Shaffer Award for Excellence as a Graduate Faculty Member, ACPA's Diamond Honoree, and ACPA's Annuit Coeptis Senior Professional Award.

Taub earned her PhD in college student personnel administration from the University of Maryland College Park, her MA in college student personnel from the University of Maryland College Park, and her BA in English from Oberlin College.